The Country Schoolmaster

Kate Grenville's bestselling novel *The Secret River* received the Commonwealth Writers' Prize and was shortlisted for the Booker Prize and the Miles Franklin Literary Award. *The Idea of Perfection* won the Women's Prize for Fiction. Grenville's other books include *Sarah Thornhill*, *The Lieutenant*, *Lilian's Story*, *Dark Places*, *Joan Makes History* and *A Room Made of Leaves*. Her 2024 novel *Restless Dolly Maunder* was shortlisted for the Women's Prize for Fiction.

Praise for Kate Grenville's *Restless Dolly Maunder*

'A work of history, biography, story and memoir, all fused into a novel that suggests the great potential of literary art as redeemer, healer and pathway to understanding . . . the writing sparkles with Grenville's gift for transcendently clear imagery'
Guardian

'Vivid and memorable . . . Grenville offers us the ambivalence and complex textures of experience without losing the rhythm and pace of realist fiction'
SARAH MOSS

'A powerful novel about a woman determined to rise above her station . . . A privilege to share in Grenville's indomitable grandmother's journey'
The Times

'Grenville . . . tells Dolly's story swiftly, cleanly and compassionately, all the while refusing to let this difficult, furious woman off the hook. Excellent'
Daily Mail

'A subversive, triumphant tale of a pioneering woman working her way through a world of limits and obstacles, who is able – despite the cost – to make a life she could call her own'
Stylist

'A memorable portrait of a proto-feminist determined to free herself from society's expectations'
Sunday Times

'Grenville astutely portrays the friction between the heroine and her daughter, who is stung by her mother's steely reserve – perhaps because she can't see the life story we've just read'
Mail on Sunday, Best New Fiction

'Brings readers into intimate acquaintance with the lives of women in late 19th- and early 20th-century rural Australia . . . elevated by Grenville's crystalline prose'
Globe and Mail

'The masterful Grenville addresses the question of why this brilliant, frustrated woman struggled to express love to her children with clarity and compassion in a swift, thoroughly absorbing book'
Mail Online

Also by Kate Grenville

Fiction

Bearded Ladies

Lilian's Story

Dreamhouse

Joan Makes History

Dark Places

The Idea of Perfection

The Secret River

The Lieutenant

Sarah Thornhill

A Room Made of Leaves

Restless Dolly Maunder

Non-fiction

The Writing Book

Making Stories (with Sue Woolfe)

Writing from Start to Finish

Searching for the Secret River

One Life: My Mother's Story

The Case Against Fragrance

Elizabeth Macarthur's Letters

The Country Schoolmaster

A Mystery in 88 Letters

Kate Grenville

CANONGATE

First published in Great Britain in 2026
by Canongate Books Ltd, 14 High Street, Edinburgh EH1 1TE

canongate.co.uk

First published in Australia in 2026 by Black Inc., an imprint of Schwartz Books Pty Ltd,
Wurundjeri Country, 22–24 Northumberland Street, Collingwood VIC 3066, Australia

1

British Library Cataloguing-in-Publication Data
A catalogue record for this book is available on
request from the British Library

ISBN 978 1 83726 803 0

Text design and typesetting by Aira Pimping

Printed and bound by CPI Group (UK) Ltd, Croydon CR0 4YY

The manufacturer's authorised representative in the EU for product safety is BGC Sustainability & Compliance, 7 avenue du Général Leclerc, Paris 75014 (gpsr@baldwinglobalconsulting.com)

FSC
www.fsc.org
MIX
Paper | Supporting responsible forestry
FSC® C013604

"If you stand right-fronting and face to face with a fact, you will see the sun glimmer on both its surfaces."

—HENRY DAVID THOREAU

Contents

PART TWO

Archive Fever

This book is an odd little thing. Partly, it's documents from the official file kept by the Department of Public Instruction about the school in Currabubula, a small village in New South Wales, in the 1880s and 1890s. There are letters, reports and transcripts of hearings. At their heart is the teacher at the one-room school and what looked like a campaign to destroy him. There'd been denunciations, accusations, nasty anonymous letters. There'd been four departmental enquiries and two court cases. He lasted under the onslaught for around ten years. Then he died.

Between these documents are my imaginings about them. It's a zig-zag journey. Was Joseph Connor the villain he was accused of being? Or was he the innocent victim of some kind of small-town vendetta, collateral damage in a war that wasn't his?

The documents are real, but the rest is story.

I came across the file more or less by accident, when I was trying to find out more about my mother. A few years after she died, I'd begun writing a sort of biography about her, and to fill in some blanks I set out on the pleasurable work of researching her life. Her parents had run pubs and she'd been a pharmacist, and the NSW State Archives had information about pubs and pharmacies.

It's a long trek out to the Archives, but I love the lucky-dip of original material, so one day I made the drive to the far western suburbs of Sydney, into a strange hinterland of high-tension wires and paddocks waiting to be made into kerbing and guttering. How you'd do research without a car I don't know – the Archives are awkward to get to by public transport and, as the website thoughtfully warns you, there are no shops within walking distance. It's a matter of bring a thermos and a sandwich.

I got through the files about pubs and pharmacies more quickly than I'd expected, and towards the end of the day I had some time left. On a whim I requested the file for Currabubula Public School. Mum's mother and father had grown up and gone to school in Currabubula, and for a year or so in the 1920s, so had she.

It was an afterthought. I didn't expect anything interesting and when the file arrived it didn't look promising. It's a couple of shabby manila folders tied up with pink tape, filled with a jumble of mostly handwritten documents. The faded ink and old handwriting make them hard to read and they're only in approximate date order. Finding anything about my grandparents or my mother seemed a hopeless task, and I was about to give it all up and go home when one piece of paper caught my eye. Maybe it was because the writing was clear and dark, and the page was the right way up. As accidental as that.

July
No. 3 Camp

Mr Inspector,
Will you be good enough to make Mr Connor learn my two children. He never learns them a bit. He takes my Lizzie

out to do his work in his kitchen, if she refuses to work for them he beats her. His wife is always telling lies of my children, getting him to beat them for nothing. They forget all Mr Boon learnt them. What Lizzie learnt in Tamworth she forgot here with them. The children have to ride fourteen miles to school, and it's not right to make them work instead of teaching them. Connor's children rob them of their lunch three days out of every week. The children get learnt nothing. He don't like any children that is not Catholics. Mr Gould sent word to me to keep the children home, they was learning nothing, but doing Connor's dirty work. We send them a long way to school, and it's not right. Everyone can tell you they learn nothing.

R. Woodbridge

I stood there holding the hundred-year-old letter with a feeling that was familiar from other archives, other bulging files of dog-eared paper. It was a blood-running-fast, itchy-palm, eyes-wide-open feeling of stumbling on something. There was a story here. But what story?

Before the Archives closed I had time to photograph a few letters, skim through the rest and scribble down some rough notes. When I got home I transferred the photos to my computer, where they joined other possibly interesting, possibly not interesting starting points for projects.

Then Covid came, and like so many others in Year One of the pandemic, I found myself in an unpleasant twilight zone that made me simultaneously restless and inert. It was out of a kind of desperation to do something – anything – that, in a lull between lockdowns, I went to the Archives again. This time I photographed every page of the file. I photographed the relevant Teachers' Files, too, and the files for all the other schools that Joseph Connor and his daughter, also a teacher, had had anything to do with.

A week later we went into lockdown again. Lockdown felt like no-time, time-out-of-time, bonus time, and that somehow gave me permission to do what seemed an obsessive, nerdy and probably pointless thing: transcribe every one of the couple of hundred documents I'd photographed.

In my experience, a book starts as a tiny corner of something you can hardly see. There's a person. And there's a situation. Usually they're based on something real. And there's a question, something you want to know. You start with those and eventually, many drafts later, you might have a story. Here I had a person, Joseph Connor, whose voice could sometimes be heard behind the bureaucratic formulas of the official letters he was writing. And there was some kind of big human drama that I didn't have a handle on. I found the documents strangely fascinating, a slice of raw life from a world that was in many ways utterly foreign, although not so far away in geography or time. And somewhere between their lines was the answer to the mystery of who Joseph Connor was, and why things had gone so badly wrong in Currabubula.

As I plunged into the file, the fascination remained, but making a narrative from it eluded me. There were too many gaps, too many unknowns, too many places where the words of the old pages flickered with ambiguity. Further research didn't yield many answers. The life of an obscure schoolmaster in a tiny country town a hundred and fifty years ago hadn't left much of a trail.

The obvious way to fill those gaps was to make things up. It would be easy enough to invent a plausible story to make sense of what was in the file. The trouble was, in shaping one story out of the slipperiness of the documents, I'd be sacrificing all the other possible stories that lay within them. I found that I absolutely didn't want to do that. In spite of all their ambiguities and gaps – or perhaps because of them – the documents had an authority that I didn't want to tamper with. Above all, they represented a poignant human reality that I seemed compelled to respect.

I was at a dead end: the documents couldn't stand alone, yet I couldn't make myself twist them into fiction. So I made up my mind to regard the puzzle of the Currabubula file as having been nothing more than an enjoyable detour from real work. Now I'd have to move on.

But ten years and several books later, I found that I was still thinking about Currabubula and the schoolmaster. The mysterious life of those documents had a hold on me that I couldn't seem to shake off. I didn't mean to return to the file, but against every sensible plan and almost against my will, I found myself sneaking back to it. I started to think of it as a bully standing in a doorway. It wasn't going to let me go through to anything else until I'd dealt with it.

All right, I thought finally, I'll chase this thing down. I'll follow every puzzle and every question, I'll give a hearing to every explanation and every story. I won't think about where I'll arrive. I'll just put one foot in front of the other, and see where I end up.

PART ONE

Currabubula Public School

Currabubula isn't a place most people have heard of. Near Tamworth, you have to say, and even that often just gets a vague nod. Northern New South Wales, you say, and their faces clear.

The village is built around Currabubula Creek, which flows through a gap in the long range that runs north to south. This was in the Country of Gomeroi people, and their name for the place sounded something like Currabubula to one of the first Europeans to see the place. When the squatters came with their sheep and cattle, the Gomeroi pushed back. They defended their homeland so effectively that, in the 1840s, many settlers abandoned their runs. But new sorts of guns, new diseases and the sheer numbers of colonists finally overwhelmed the Gomeroi and for long oppressed decades they were an embattled people, living on the margins of the white world but never losing their sense of themselves and their connection to their Country.

By 1880, Currabubula was a small village servicing an area of family farms. It had a pub, a blacksmith, a butcher, a general store, a post office in the back of the hotel and a railway service that picked up and delivered mail. The nearest school was a few hours' ride away, in the big town of Tamworth.

That year the government passed a new *Public Instruction Act*. It made schooling free, or virtually free, where previously families had to pay. The Act also made publicly funded education secular, where previously most schools were run by churches. And, most radically of all, the Act made school compulsory for all children between the ages of six and fourteen, when before that education had been the privilege of a minority. The government undertook to provide a schoolhouse, a teacher and equipment for any place that could guarantee twenty pupils.

Almost before the ink was dry on the Act, a committee of Currabubula men got together and applied. Currabubula Public School opened in 1882 with fifty-six pupils. The original schoolhouse is still there, added to but not much changed: a solid little brick building with some decorative brickwork around the windows. The creek curves around the end of a big sloping playground. Hard up against the school building is the teacher's cottage, modest of size and plain of face.

The first teacher was William Boon. He was there for two years. Then he was transferred to another school and Joseph Connor took over. He was thirty-nine years old when he arrived in Currabubula. For the previous six years he'd been teaching at two small schools in the backblocks of New England. The transfer to Currabubula was a promotion: a bigger school, big enough to warrant a pupil-teacher to share the teacher's load. Not too far from Tamworth, with all that a fair-sized town had to offer. On the train line. Just looking at the file, you can see that Joseph Connor was a man on the up-and-up.

In the Archives there's a photo of the pupils and teacher of Currabubula Public School, taken a few years after Connor arrived. The kids are all lined up beside the school building: close to seventy of them, by my count. It's hard to make out detail, but you can see that the better-dressed children are in the front row, sitting apart from the less well-put-together children crammed in further back.

Three adults stand at the end of the row: two women and between them a man who must be Joseph Connor. In the photo he's just an impression of a tall, solid, broad-shouldered man, his face half hidden by a beard. Something about the graceless way he's standing tells you he'd be one of those big men awkward with their own legs and arms, whose clothes never seem to fit quite right. But maybe that suggestion of fluster was just the moment the photo was taken. After all, he's just herded seventy-odd children into some kind of order so the camera can see them all, explained how they mustn't move – imagine trying to persuade a great crowd of kids not to move! – and tried to steady the toddler at his knees who's now immortalised as a grey smudge.

The photo didn't tell me much about him, but in that last trawl through the Archives I'd called up the files for his two previous schools. The first one had a copy of the form he'd filled in when he applied to be a teacher, six years before arriving in Currabubula.

11th June 1878
Applicant: Joseph Connor

<u>State the particulars of your early education</u>
I was first taught in a National School in Ireland, for a term of six or seven years. At the termination of that time, I was sent to a training school at which I remained about twelve months.

How has your time been occupied since you were 18 years of age?

I was about thirteen years a goldminer. I was twelve months teaching a school. About three years doing various kinds of manual labour.

How are your evenings at present spent?

Teaching a night school.

Have you ever been trained as a teacher? If so, state the particulars.

I have. In the Model School of Dunmanway, County of Cork, Ireland.

If you have ever been engaged in teaching, state explicitly where, how long, and under what circumstances.

I taught as second teacher in a National School in Victoria for a term of three months. I taught a private school near Coonamble for twelve months. I have been teaching a night school for the past seven weeks in Inverell.

If you have discontinued teaching, state your reasons for doing so.

I discontinued teaching in Victoria to go to the goldfields. I was discharged from the school in Coonamble in consequence of the drought.

State what you think the moral qualifications of a teacher should be – for instance, as regards Industry, Conscientiousness, Uprightness, Temperance.

I am of opinion that a teacher should be industrious and set a good example to his pupils in every way. He should be strictly honest in all his dealings and he should refrain from intoxicating liquors.

What is your present means of subsistence?

Getting firewood in the daytime, and at night teaching a school.

signed, Joseph Connor

11th July 1878

Report by Inspector on Joseph Connor, applicant for the office of teacher.

Age: 33 years
Married or otherwise: married
Place where born: Ireland
Religious denomination: Roman Catholic
Personal appearance: good
Constitution: good
Bodily infirmities: none
Apparent character: intelligent and active
Attainments:
    Reading – fair
    Writing – tolerable
    Arithmetic – fair
    Grammar – fair
    Geography – fair+
    School management – tolerable
    Dictation – tolerable
    Aptitude for teaching – fair

I have to read this twice, because it doesn't seem to make sense. On the second read I realise that's because I've come to it with a stereotype of a nineteenth-century schoolmaster, and it doesn't fit with what I'm seeing here. What I've got in my mind is a clean-shaven beaky-nosed man with rimless glasses, a tidy haircut, a patrician face above a high starched collar, and a stern imperious look. A man of learning, well spoken, what you might call a gentleman, with a stick in his hand to point at the long division on the blackboard. But what's here is no buttoned-up gentleman with glasses flashing in the light. Joseph Connor only had *six or seven* years of schooling himself. His reading and writing are only *tolerable* – Departmental code for a bare pass. This is a man who's spent most of his adult life as a gold miner. Now he's a wood-carter with a side-hustle teaching the rudiments of literacy to a few adults.

But Joseph Connor timed his application well, because in 1878 the Department of Public Instruction was desperate for teachers. Teaching was a good job: clean desk work, a lifetime's secure employment, a salary of something like 300 pounds a year and a pension at the end of it. All he had to do was play by the Department's rules.

On Connor's left in the photo is a woman in a dark dress. This must be his wife, Ann. She's standing a bit tilted, holding the white shape of a baby. The baby looks heavy – you can see she's straining to keep hoisting it up for the camera.

On his right is another woman in an even darker dress. She's standing rigidly at attention, her feet neatly together, hands folded tidily at her waist. She looks like a person wanting very much to be doing the right thing. She's looking at the camera, but the old photo is too faint to make out her face. This would be the pupil-teacher, I think – Joseph Connor's apprentice.

At the other end of the long row of pupils is another young woman. She doesn't look like the other girls – they're all wearing white pinafores over dark dresses, where she's wearing a long light-coloured dress, and she's standing, while the others are sitting. She's glancing down, the only person in the photograph not looking at the camera. This is probably Joseph Connor's daughter Bridget (known as Bridie), aged thirteen or fourteen.

I get out my magnifying glass and peer at all the faces, but all I can do is make the blurs bigger. Does Joseph Connor look like a man who *beat his pupils*? Does his wife look like a woman who *told lies about them*? Does the pupil-teacher really look as if she wants to be a schoolteacher? What's Bridie thinking as she turns away from the camera? And why on earth am I so interested in these strangers?

The Pleasure of the Minister

I pore over the first few letters in the file from Connor to the Department of Public Instruction. They're trivial, but I know that somewhere not too far down the track, Connor is going to be the subject of that vitriolic letter. So I'm teasing apart every tiny fibre of these documents, hoping they'll tell me something more than they seem to.

26th July 1884
Joseph Connor to Inspector Jones

Sir,
I have the honour to apply for travelling expenses for myself family and luggage from Fernhill Public School to here during the present month.

List of expenses incurred by J. Connor and family in proceeding from Fernhill Public School to Currabubula Public School in July, 1884.

Buggy hire from Fernhill to Inverell	15/-
Dalworth's coach, Inverell to Glen Innes	4/-/-
Cobb & Co coach Glen Innes to Armidale	7/-/-
Railway fares, Armidale to Currabubula	2/5/-
Meals and beds	1/18/-

Luggage, Fernhill to Inverell		7/6
"	Inverell to Uralla	1/5/6
"	Uralla to Currabubula	14/6

Total eighteen pounds, fifteen shillings and six pence.

I have etc.
J. Connor

Now that trip would take less than a day. For Connor and his wife and five children, it was a couple of days of travel and at least one night in lodgings. The buggy. Then the local coach. Then the Cobb & Co coach. Then the train.

I picture him totting it all up – no calculator, of course – the sums in a tidy line down the page. Easy to make a mistake with the pennies and the shillings and the pounds. He's a little frightened at the size of the total. A man could cart wood for a couple of months before he earned that much.

He double-checks it. At the Department he knows there'll be a clerk whose job it is to check the teachers' sums. Connor's been told that the costs of the Department of Public Instruction are now the *largest single drain on the public purse*. He knows plenty of folk think that providing an education for every child is money thrown away.

At Fernhill, before he got the hang of things, he'd had something close to trouble with the Department. He'd asked for money to build a horse enclosure for the children who rode in to school. He'd dodged being *censured* but the local Inspector told him it was a near thing. It'll be the end of me, he thinks, if I do the sum wrong and overcharge!

Inspector Jones thriftily writes his reply at the bottom of the same piece of paper.

> Mr Connor, applicants for removal are not allowed travelling expenses. Did you not apply for removal from Fernhill? Please note below.
>
> J. Stephen Jones, 3-8-84

Removal is one of the Department's many technical terms. It means that the Department has assigned you to another school. However, *applicants for removal* requested the change themselves, and in that case the Department doesn't pay for your expenses.

Connor feels a spurt of irritation. The tone is distrustful. They're suspicious of us Irish, he thinks. Got us all marked for drunkards and crooks. He's annoyed with himself too. He should have taken more care, spelled it out. Now he's wasted the Inspector's time. His reply will have to be carefully done to remedy the bad start, but it's impossible to think in the din of the little house: the baby grizzling on and on, teething of course, Ann and Bridie doing the bread for the morning, the boys squabbling, and little Roland lurching about too close to the stove so Bridie shouts and grabs him and Ann drops the lump of dough she's been kneading, bang on the dusty floor. He can already feel the grit in tomorrow's bread.

Next door in the schoolroom, lantern at his elbow, he can get down to his reply. It's got to lay out the facts, be economical of words and do a bit of buttering-up as well. Something tells me he does a couple of drafts. He's got to make the thing clear and be quick about it, but most of all he's got to get the money. By God, he thinks, they won't cheat me of what I'm owed!

There's not enough space underneath the Inspector's frosty little reply. He has to turn the page over and finish it on the back, but he makes sure to break the sentence in the middle so the continuation can't be missed.

Sir,

In reply to the above I beg to state that I was not a candidate for removal. About three months ago I applied for removal to the Bundarra Public School, but I did not get the appointment on account of the appointment having been made before my letter had been received at the Dept. of Pubc. Inst. Since then I made no application for removal but waited the pleasure of the Minister, knowing that my classification would procure me an appointment to a better school in due time.

J. Connor, 4-8-84

Waited the pleasure of the Minister. I'm imagining him sitting back, pleased. A bit feudal, he thinks. They like that. And the humble pie of *knowing that my classification would procure me an appointment to a better school in due time.*

Joseph Connor has a big, clear, rather unsophisticated hand that takes up plenty of space. It's a bit like the man with the beard in the photo – loose and rangy. But not so loose and rangy that he doesn't know how to work the system. I'm feeling him as a canny fellow, someone who knows how to play the Department's game. The stakes are high. He doesn't want to go back to carting wood. His reply makes him sound like a bit of a suck-up, but that's understandable.

I'm getting a picture of him, but I might be squeezing this bland little exchange for more juice than it really has. I'm looking for that man who seems to have been hounded to his grave. But official correspondence probably isn't the right place to go looking for a human being.

On his first morning at Currabubula, Connor would have seen how overcrowded the schoolroom was. It was built to accommodate the fifty-six children whose parents had applied for it. But that was two years earlier, and now there are seventy children on the class roll, the numbers recently swelled by his own three school-age children. The pupils are packed in so tightly along the benches that they can hardly raise their arms to write on their slates. Some of the bigger boys have to stand, leaning against the walls, and there's a clutch of little ones sitting on the rough-sawn floorboards. As the day goes on, Connor has to make sure the children take it in turns to have a seat.

I'll have to get some planks, cobble together a few more benches, he thinks. The big boys fill a lot of space – in the photo, three of them are as tall as he is. They jostle together near his desk at the front of the room. The little ones wriggle and pinch each other.

Within a week of Connor taking over from William Boon, two parents come to him after school. George Morris owns the pub that his father established back in the 1840s. The Morris Hotel is the only big building in the village, and the main thoroughfare in the village is called Morris Street. Connor understands straight away that Morris is more or less the king of little Currabubula. John Giles owns a prosperous farm near the village. He's a man of some education – he'd organised the application to set up the school four years earlier and now he's sending three children along. He's a vigorous, call-a-spade-a-shovel kind of man.

Morris lets Giles do the talking. It's a disgrace, he says. They'll have to extend the schoolroom, no two ways about it. You'll have to write, Connor. To the Minister. Boon said he would, but he didn't have … Giles pauses and Connor knows he's thinking, *Didn't have the balls to do it.* Couldn't see his way clear, he finishes.

Morris and Giles both watch Connor. Judging the size of his balls.

Connor knows the Department will never agree to enlarge the schoolroom. Now that schooling is compulsory, every school in New South Wales is bursting at the seams. He knows the letter will end up on the desk of the local Inspector, and there's already been that little smear of trouble about the removal expenses. Connor doesn't want to get a name for pestering. But he can't afford to get these two offside.

He suggests the request would be better coming from them – that the Department will respond well to a letter from the *leading men in the community*. Laying on a bit of flattery won't do any harm, he thinks. He promises he'll let them see the teacher's register so they can quote the exact numbers.

28th September 1884

John Giles to the Minister for Public Instruction

Sir,

I am requested by the parents of the children attending the Public School at this place to call your attention to the insufficient accommodation in the school room. There is only seating accommodation for 56 children and there are nearly 70 in attendance at times and those over the number of 56 had to stand until provided with temporary seats by the Teacher.

The building in the first instance was only put up to hold 56 children. Consequently all over that number are occupying the space left for the Teacher thereby putting him to inconvenience for want of space and the danger of children being too close packed in summer is not to be lost sight of by parents.

Trusting you will give this important matter your earliest attention.

I remain, Sir, your most obedient servant
John Giles

29th September 1884
Inspector Jones to District Inspector Miller

Sir,
Upon inquiry I find that the average attendance at Currabubula is 56 and the number of cubic feet for each child 119.

The Act states that there is to be "an apportionment of space not less than 100 cubic feet for each child ordinarily in attendance".

Under these circumstances I would recommend that Mr Giles be informed that there is already sufficient breathing space for the number of children in average attendance at Currabubula and his application for the enlargement of the Public School at Currabubula must be declined.

J. Stephen Jones

There they are in Connor's kitchen, George Morris and John Giles and Joseph Connor, a copy of the letter from J. Stephen Jones on the table between them. Does Connor laugh when he gets to *sufficient breathing space*, the way I did?

Morris and Giles don't see anything funny about the business of cubic feet of air. They're cranky. They've never worked for anyone but themselves. These are men used to getting their own way.

Later, there's Connor out in the yard in the dusk splitting firewood, his shadow a long lean thing against the fence as he raises the axe, brings it down. The satisfying clunk as the wood cleaves along its grain and falls in two pieces. In the house the baby is wailing, the toddler screaming – he knows just how the child looks, red in the face, lying on the floor kicking – the next one up sneaking a handful of dried dates while Mother's not looking. He hears Bridie call out sharply – even at ten she can already put the edge on her voice that he hears in his own, all day long in the classroom. The hubbub stops.

He doesn't mind being out here in the quiet with the wood and the axe, nice and sharp, the handle smooth and obedient in his hands. Morris and Giles will keep on at him, so he'll write. But not to the Minister, and not about getting a bigger schoolroom.

He brings the axe down into the block, picks up an armful of wood. Near dark now, the kitchen window full of golden lamplight and things mercifully quiet.

Giles has done his dash, done the big I-am. Now he'll step in himself. Ask, but not for too much. That was the trick of it. Never ask for so much that they'll have to say no.

30th October 1884
Joseph Connor to Inspector Jones

Sir,
I beg to inform you that I have made inquiries as to the probable cost of the two forms for seating required for use in this school.
Mr Bussell of Tamworth states that he can make them for 14/- each, that is of the usual size, about 8ft long and 15 inches high.

I have the honour etc.
Joseph Connor

31st October 1884
Inspector Jones to Joseph Connor

Mr Connor,

1. How many forms are there at present in this school?
2. What is the exact length of each form & how many scholars will each form accommodate?
3. What is the average daily attendance of your pupils?

J. Stephen Jones

2nd November 1884
Joseph Connor to Inspector Jones

Mr Inspector Jones,

1. There are 9 forms at present at the school
2. Each form is 8 feet long and will not accommodate more than 5 pupils with comfort.
3. The average daily attendance for last week was 58.9. This week so far is 64.

J. Connor

The dim coolness of the tiled bar of the Albion, the best pub in Tamworth. Connor and Inspector Jones sitting at a little table with their beers.

John Jones, a man who's found a way to give his insultingly ordinary name a bit of heft, is divided in his soul by the contradictory demands of his job. Twenty years' employment at the Department has taught him that being seen as thrifty is the way to promotion. But his job is to make the schools in his charge run efficiently as well as cheaply. A classroom full of hulking boys – *scholars!* – lounging against the walls and little ones getting splinters in their backsides … well, if the District Inspector should happen to drop in to Currabubula Public School, the local Inspector who presided over that situation could look remiss.

> **3rd November 1884**
> Inspector Jones to District Inspector Miller
>
> Two more forms are much required at Currabubula. Mr Connor told me personally the other day in Tamworth, that his little ones have to take it <u>in turns</u> to sit down. This must be very trying this warm weather.
>
> I would recommend that permission be granted to order Mr Bussell to make two forms 8 ft long and 15 inches high, and to send them to Currabubula by train. The cost of forms and carriage not to exceed 35/-.
>
> J. Stephen Jones

Connor calls into John Giles's place.

Applied the soft soap, Giles, he says. Laughs, pleased with himself. Not for a bigger place, no joy in that. But your lads will have somewhere to sit at least.

Ah, that's a good start, Giles says, shaking his hand, all forgiven. Now there's my man. You and your Irish blarney!

That's how I'm picturing it, anyway. A man congratulating himself on dealing neatly with his first dilemma.

Along with not enough seats and too many pupils, when Joseph Connor took over at Currabubula he inherited a pupil-teacher, Miss Mercy Stuckey. His predecessor, Mr Boon, had been enthusiastic about her, reporting that she *appears to be strong and well qualified in every respect*, and praising her *cheerful and ready willingness*. He assessed her moral character as *very good, judging from observations made while not under school restraint.*

Something about that last phrase summons a sudden vivid picture in my mind: Mr Boon, a young man of twenty-five, working alongside fifteen-year-old Mercy Stuckey. Close quarters in the small crowded schoolroom, day after day. Then after school, sitting side by side at the teacher's table while he gives her extra lessons. She'll need those to pass the exams that will qualify her to become a teacher. The quiet room, the stove crackling away, their faces soft in the lamplight, heads bowed together over the sentence to be parsed, the long division to be worked. *Observations made while not under school restraint. Cheerful and ready willingness.* Is it just me, or is Mr Boon saying more than he realises?

Joseph Connor had been at Currabubula for a month when he made out his own report on Miss Stuckey.

15th August 1884

Teacher's Report upon Miss Mercy Stuckey, age 15, pupil-teacher

Health – It should here be stated whether the pupil-teacher suffers from any physical infirmity likely to interfere with the discharge of duty, and whether any symptoms of failure in health have been remarked since appointment. It should also be specified if leave of absence has been obtained, and on what plea, as well as for how long.

Miss Stuckey appears to be in good health. I have noticed no symptoms of failure in her health whilst I have been in charge of this school. My predecessor informed me that he noticed nothing amiss with her health. Miss Stuckey has never applied for leave of absence. She has not been absent on any school day since the date of my taking charge.

Conduct out of school: Special reference should be given to moral character, as evidenced by the persons chosen as associates, and the mode of spending leisure time.

Miss Stuckey's moral character appears to me to be quite blameless. I have not seen her in the company of any but respectable persons.

Conduct in school: The points requiring particular remark are punctuality, obedience and attention to duty.

Miss Stuckey is very punctual and fairly diligent. As regards obedience she follows her instructions faithfully and she pays constant attention to her duty.

Diligence in home study: Miss Stuckey pays much attention to her home lessons.

Progress since last examination: Miss Stuckey has made very fair progress during the short time I have been in charge of the school.

Efficiency and usefulness: Miss Stuckey is fairly efficient and useful. I perceive a marked improvement in her method of teaching since the 18th July ult., the date of my taking charge here.

signed, J. Connor

It strikes me that this report is actually about Joseph Connor as much as it's about Mercy Stuckey. He doesn't say that she's healthy, only that she *appears* to be. And if it turns out she isn't, he can shift the blame to Boon, who's told him that he's noticed nothing amiss. As for her moral character, he'll only say that she *appears* quite blameless. She's *very* punctual, but only *fairly* diligent. It's like a having-it-both-ways forecast that says there's *a chance of rain*.

And at the end, he goes beyond what the form asks for, something that not only puts him at the centre of the picture but also gives himself a little golden radiance of virtue: *I perceive a marked improvement since the date of my taking charge here.*

I'm squeamish about this tone of self-advertisement. A bit embarrassed for him, toadying up to his masters at the Department. But I suppose I shouldn't be. He's been lucky, getting the job at a time when no one was looking too closely at qualifications. He's already been moved up the ladder and he'd have his eye on more promotions. Bigger schools, more pay. Maybe one day he'll even get out of the bearpit of the classroom and follow Inspector Jones to a desk job. He's got a family to support, five human beings who without the money he earns would literally go hungry. It's another twenty-four years before the first inklings of a minimum wage, fifty before unemployment benefits. Fifty-eight before pensions for widows, if he should die. No wonder he's grovelling.

I'm liking him, this canny Irishman. He's in a harsh system but you can see him working out how to use it. I picture him smiling into his beard as he thinks of another way to polish his halo, and I'm smiling too, at the picture I'm making of him.

Accouchement

19th March 1885
Joseph Connor to Inspector Jones

Sir,
I beg to request that Mrs Connor be exempted from teaching needlework for one month from this date in consequence of her accouchement.

I have etc.
J. Connor, Teacher

When I was peering at the photo of the school I thought the white bundle of baby that Ann was holding on her hip might help me date the photo. After I'd spent some time with the Births, Deaths and Marriages registry I could see it wasn't going to, because Ann Connor always had a baby on her hip. There were already five children, plus a firstborn who'd died in infancy.

The new baby would be a girl, and they'd call her Abigail.

A Low Mean Dirty Lot

Now I've come to where I started. Joseph Connor has been in Curra-bubula for just on a year, and Inspector Jones receives the poisonous letters. Two of them.

July 1885
Robert Woodbridge to Inspector Jones
No. 3 Camp

Mr Inspector
Will you be good enough to make Mr Connor learn my two children. He never learns them a bit. He takes my Lizzie out to do his work in his kitchen, if she refuses to work for them he beats her. His wife is always telling lies of my children, getting him to beat them for nothing. They forget all Mr Boon learnt them. What Lizzie learnt in Tamworth she forgot here with them. The children have to ride fourteen miles to school, and it's not right to make them work instead of teaching them. Connor's children rob them of their lunch three days out of every week. The children get learnt nothing. He don't like any children that is not Catholics. Mr Gould sent word to me to keep the children home, they was learning nothing, but doing Connor's dirty work. We send them a long way to

school, and it's not right. Everyone can tell you they learn nothing.

R. Woodbridge

July 1885

John Giles to Inspector Jones

Sir,

This is to let you know I am not going to send my children back to the school while Connor is in it they learn nothing and only forget all good Mr Boon taught them. All the people are dissatisfied with Connor. Gould told me he would get him shifted for us in June so he is gone I ask you to shift him on behalf of the people the children are out playing nearly all day the constable and old Mrs Morris have timed them out for one hour at eleven and other times Connor is out with visitors all day. His house is full of people all day and all night. No respectable man or woman will be seen at his place he never keeps the Sabbath day. He has a low lot at the school cricketing and roundering and all the people can tell you his wife washes her clothes on Sunday she is a low dirty bad woman Mr Gould has to take pity on the dirty school and clean it and feed the hungry children. Connor steal all the children's lunches. Only for kind Mr Gould there would be no children going to it so a lot are leaving Connor told Gould and Mr Deighton that he had you under his thumb to give him good marks and to promote him and I said he don't serve good marks he learns them nothing and they are a low mean dirty lot, shunned and hated by every one, not fit to teach blacks. Give us back good Mr Boon who pleased every one and done his duty to the poor children.

I remain yours,
The Voice of the People
J. Giles

The following month there are these two:

18th August 1885
John Giles to the Minister for Education

I, John Giles, farmer, Currabubula, do most solemnly and sincerely declare that I did not write the letter produced & signed J. Giles, and that I know nothing of the complaints contained therein.

I have no complaints whatever to make against the teacher.

John Giles

18th August 1885
Robert Woodbridge to the Minister of Education

I, Robert Woodbridge, employed on the Railway no. 3 camp, do most solemnly and sincerely declare that I did not write the letter produced & signed R. Woodbridge, and that I know nothing of the complaints contained therein.

I have no complaints whatever to make against the teacher.

Robert Woodbridge

When I initially skimmed Robert Woodbridge's letter, that first day at the Archives, I wanted to know why he was so cranky about Connor, and whether his accusations were fair. Once I read the file properly, it became clear that Woodbridge didn't have a problem with Connor, and nor did John Giles.

But someone did. That person had such a problem with Connor that they'd written two letters, and even gone to the trouble of making them sound as if they were from different men, repeating some accusations but coming up with different ones as well.

That person must have known the letters would quickly be identified as forgeries. But until they were, everyone who read them would think they were written by two respectable citizens whose opinions counted. That person would have known that once mud has been flung, some of it sticks.

The litany of complaints in the letters is completely at odds with the man I've been constructing in my imagination. That man who doesn't miss a chance to suck up, who's so careful to stay on the right side of the Department – does he really not *learn* any of his pupils? That woman, that dim, weary figure holding a baby – can she really be a tyrant who makes Lizzie Woodbridge do her housework, and gets her husband to *beat her* if she says no?

That throwaway line about Connor being *not fit to teach blacks* sends me back to the old photo. I peer with a magnifying glass, looking for kids with darker skin. I can't see any in the blurry crowd, but Aboriginal children might be there, with or without darker skin. Or they might not be: back then, if a white parent objected to the presence of Aboriginal pupils, the school was allowed to turn them away. Maybe that had happened at Currabubula, to make that school photo so very white.

In any case I'm thinking about the accusations. They sound pretty damning, but there might be more to the story. *What Lizzie learnt in Tamworth she forgot here with them.* That could be true. But it mightn't be Joseph Connor's fault. Lizzie Woodbridge is nine and the work's getting harder. She's falling behind and her father's rousing on her. She's come up with a story that gets him off her back – blame the teacher.

The children are out playing nearly all day – yes, that might be how it looks. But Joseph Connor has seventy kids in a room made for fifty-six. He's probably staggering the recess and lunchtimes. It might seem as though children are out all the time, but if you looked closely you'd see they were different kids at different times.

He takes my Lizzie out to do his work in the kitchen – that could be true, too, and it sounds bad, until you remember how crowded the schoolroom is. It's sensible for Mrs Connor to take the girls into the house for the needlework lessons, but she's got the baby and the toddler with her, so she gets the older girls to take turns keeping the children distracted while she shows the others how to do blanket stitch.

As for *his wife washes her clothes on Sunday* – you tell me, Mr Accuser, with eight people in the house, including several little kids and at least one in nappies, can Mrs Connor be choosy about when she does the washing?

I feel myself bristling up in Joseph Connor's defence. It's as if I've got one of those shape-sorting toys, where children push the square thing through the square hole and the triangular thing through the triangular hole. I'm turning everything I read around in my mind until it fits through that pro-Connor-shaped hole. Why am I doing that? I think it might be because of memories from my own schooldays.

I suppose most kids can be horrors in the classroom, but I was a particular kind of horror. In high school I kept a notebook under my desk. On the cover I wrote TEACHERISMS, and inside I made notes about the peculiarities of the women (and one man) who taught us. I made notes about their mistakes and their slips of the tongue. I recorded the cruel nicknames we'd given them. I mocked the way they looked and the way they dressed. The one who was forever plunging a hand down into her neckline to drag up a bra strap. The one whose favourite brooch looked like a blob of chewed caramel.

If you were being grand, I suppose you could say I was practising for writing novels. I was doing what I later read that Henry James said that a writer must do: *observe perpetually*. And I suppose that, compared to the kids with knives in some of today's classrooms, a nasty notebook is small beer. But I'm deeply ashamed now. I was making the lives of those teachers – most of whom I actually liked a lot – even more stressful and difficult than they already were. I think that might be what I'm bringing to my efforts to understand Joseph Connor: shame, and a good dose of sympathy.

Now that I've countered the accusations to my satisfaction, I'm trying to work out what might have motivated the accuser. Could it be the Catholic thing? *He don't like any children that is not Catholics.* The divide between Catholics and Protestants was certainly a big deal in the past, but I don't think it's behind these letters. For a start, John Giles, like roughly a third of the school's parents, was Catholic. I haven't been able to find out whether Robert Woodbridge was too. But if the accuser was motivated by sectarianism, he'd surely have picked two Protestant fathers to impersonate. And apart from that one sentence, none of the criticisms is about Connor discriminating against non-Catholic pupils. That's a dead end.

But I am noticing a recurring theme in both letters: *good Mr Boon*. Perhaps he somehow lies at the bottom of these peculiar forgeries. What was so good about him?

According to the Teachers' File, William Boon wasn't actually all that good. He *incurred the Minister's severe displeasure* and was *censured* several times. In fact, he was nearly sacked. The standard of his teaching was poor, he caned the children too much and he was sloppy about collecting school fees. The Department didn't think he had much to recommend him, so why was the writer of those letters so keen to get him back?

One document suggests a possible answer:

23rd December 1882
William Boon to the Under-Secretary, Department of Public Instruction

Sir, in accordance with my instructions, I have the honour to submit the following return of the number of pupils enrolled at the school under my charge for each of the four weeks ending 22nd Dec 1882, also the average attendance for the same period.

Week ending Dec 1st: Enrolled 31, average attendance 26.8
Week ending Dec 8th: Enrolled 43, average attendance 28.4
Week ending Dec 14th: Enrolled 47, average attendance 28.3
Week ending Dec 25th: Enrolled 59, average attendance 34.4

Owing to harvesting operations, the attendance during the above period has been very irregular.

W. Boon
Teacher

I remember from primary school the ritual of the roll call. Mrs Linney up the front, the alphabetical list. I'd be waiting for the name of my friend Caroline Gardiner because I'd be next. *Present!* The strange seriousness of it, the call and response: a solemn churchy sort of feel. Mrs Linney with a little furrow between her eyebrows, uncharacteristically anxious and tetchy. Her panic on the morning she marked Alison Maxwell present when she was really absent.

I know now that the Teacher's Roll is a significant legal document. Parents are obliged by law to send their children to school and the roll is the official record of attendance. But Mr Boon would have known that the small farmers around Currabubula had always depended on the free labour of their children and often needed to keep them home. In the days before cheap fencing wire, a man with sheep needed shepherds, and even quite young children make good shepherds. A man with a crop of wheat needed it to be harvested and bagged. A man's meals had to be cooked and served in a labour-intensive world without running water, electricity or supermarkets. Compulsory education meant that, virtually overnight, all those small farms lost the unpaid workers who made the whole thing possible. The Act meant financial disaster for many, but there'd been no consultation and no compensation. Unsurprisingly, in some quarters the reform was resented.

During December 1882, marking all those absences on the roll every morning, William Boon knows that the absent children are at home sewing up wheat bags. But he can see the parents' point of view, and he doesn't want them to get a visit from the Attendance Officer. In adding that disclaimer to the attendance record, he's implicitly appealing to his masters to be understanding. That was at some risk to himself. His job was to enforce the Act, not to defend the parents. Whereas the picture I'm getting of Joseph Connor is of a man careful of his standing with the Department. Not a man to turn a blind eye at harvest time. Mr Accuser might be thinking that if Joseph Connor was criticised enough, the Department would move him, and with luck his replacement would be someone as easygoing as William Boon. In that case, the real anger is about the Act, not about Joseph Connor.

As an explanation this feels a bit far-fetched, but it makes sense of the forged letters and I'm glad of that. It means I can go on feeling sympathetic towards poor conscientious Joseph Connor.

19th August 1885
Inspector Jones to the Chief Inspector

Sir,
Mssrs John Giles, Currabubula, and Robert Woodbridge, No. 3 Camp, did not write these letters or attach their signatures thereto. They have no complaints whatever to make against the Teacher, so they must have been written by some malicious & evil spirited person in Currabubula or neighbourhood. There are no other persons of the same name in the locality.

I have made my inquiry and cannot find out the perpetrator & do not believe there is any foundation for said complaints.

J. Stephen Jones
Inspector

Oh, *some malicious and evil spirited person*! I suppose it's possible that someone got a kick out of forging these letters, but it seems at least as far-fetched an explanation as mine. It sounds as if the Inspector just wants this whole nasty little episode – which is drawing the Department's attention to one of his schools in an unwelcome way – to disappear.

25th August 1885
Petition to the Minister for Public Instruction

Honourable Sir,
Having been informed of the investigations recently held by you in regard to some complaints laid against

Mr Connor, Teacher of this place, which complaints are as you are aware forgeries, we the undersigned have called a public meeting to express our heartfelt sympathy with Mr & Mrs Connor. We have much pleasure Sir in assuring you that Mr Connor is extremely popular here both as a Teacher and as a member of our community; we are quite certain that he has given no cause for this cowardly attack on his character and we are equally certain that he has no enemies excepting the base author of these forgeries.

We should feel very much obliged to you Sir should you assure the District Inspector of our entire confidence in Mr Connor.

We have the honour to inform you Sir that during the past five or six years almost every member of this community have been at one time or the other subjected to the annoyance of scurrilous writings from some evil disposed family who appear to find much pleasure in persecuting their neighbours.

We have the honour Sir to subscribe ourselves
Yours, very respectfully

Maurice Deighton
Mary Deighton
George Morris
Mary Morris
Charles Whyman
Rebecca Whyman
Michael McCarthy
Nora McCarthy
John McCarthy
Bridget McCarthy
James McCarthy
J.W.C. Griffin
William Griffin
J.P. Moorby
Alfred Gould
Annie Gould
Mary Fuller
G.H. Sinclair
Ellen Sinclair
George Lindley
James Bollard
William Sugden
Elizabeth Sugden
Christopher Kelly
Margaret Kelly
Mary Boots
Michael Minogue
John Hawthorne
Margaret Hawthorne
William Bollard
George Wright
Elizabeth Wright

Daniel Manning
Margaret Manning
Robert Goodsir
C. Goodsir
James A. Wright
Edwin Reynold
Jonathan Griffin
Ernest Cotterill
Ada Cotterill
William Wright
Mary Wright
C.A. Cheetham
A.J. Cotterill
Michael Sheridan
John Giles
Jane Giles
Francis McLachlan
John Howarth
Michael McCarthy
Rose McCarthy

Noted, J. Connor 31-8-85

From the sound of this, Deighton and Morris know who wrote the letters. If they didn't, they wouldn't say evil-disposed *family*, would they? They'd be more likely to say evil-disposed *person*. So this sounds like a genuine explanation of what's happening, in which case my story about people resenting the government is too elaborate. This is starting to taking shape as one of those stories that happen in isolated communities: some ancient dispute over missing cattle or ambiguous boundary lines – the feud going on for years, the original argument lost to time, only the malice still full of life, the hostility fuelled by the strange toxic things that happen when people are locked in with each other and no one's got enough of anything: education, money, power, respect. In that story, the writer's real targets might have been R. Woodbridge and J. Giles rather than Joseph Connor. Respectable John Giles, Chair of the School Committee and all-round pillar of the community, wouldn't have liked being mocked as *The Voice of the People.*

I'm glad to see Connor's squiggle on the bottom. I'd like to know how he felt when they showed him the petition. Were there tears in his eyes as he saw all those people on his side? Or was he too angry to be comforted? There might have been a pulse of relief, too, that the Department wouldn't come nosing around to see exactly how he was managing his school. No teacher is perfect, after all, and Joseph Connor had only just squeaked into the profession.

These nasty letters don't tell me anything about him. He wasn't a villain, and he wasn't really a victim either. It was just his turn to get a scurrilous letter.

Still, I find myself going back to those forged notes. I have trouble trying to imagine the *malicious family* scenario, because on a further look it seems unlikely. The fifty-odd people who signed the petition are a large proportion of this little community. Everyone knows everyone else. Their children play together. Their parents and grandparents knew each other. They're the best part of a day's ride from the nearest town and everyone's dependent on the others for help when it's needed. Yet one family – not a crackpot individual but a whole family – has made itself a pariah by churning out *scurrilous writings* against *almost every* neighbour. That's weird. Actually, it's a bit hard to believe.

And the accusations are oddly specific. If you were just getting a kick out of being malicious, would you mention by name those real men in the village, Gould and Deighton, and think up the surely peculiar assertion that Mr Gould cleaned the school and *sent word to keep the children home*? Would you name a date when Gould promised he'd get rid of Connor? If you just wanted to make trouble, would you invent that hard-to-imagine business about Connor stealing the pupils' lunches? And surely you'd just say that the children were wasting their time, rather than naming the specific ways they did it – *cricketing and roundering* – and the particular, named individual – Old Mrs Morris – who had her watch in her hand to *time them out*.

Perhaps these are the frills a good storyteller invents to make a tale come to life. Or perhaps they have the oddness of truth.

J. Stephen Jones and the petitioners are sure that Joseph Connor is innocent, and I was too. I'd made up my mind, back on that day in the Archives with the forged letters in my hand, and if there's one thing harder than knowing the truth of a situation, it's changing your mind about it. But the more I turn the thing over, the less convinced I become. There's a little buckle of unease in my picture of poor put-upon Joseph Connor. Plus, unlike those people who signed the petition, I've read the file. I know there's more trouble ahead.

Accouchement

10th January 1887
Joseph Connor to Inspector Jones

Sir,
I have the honour to ask for leave of absence for Mrs Connor for one month from this date, from the teaching of needlework at this school on account of her accouchement.

I have the honour etc.
J. Connor

Adophus was born in February. He was the seventh living Connor child. Above him was Abigail, two years old, then James, four, Roland six, Ernest, eight, Alfred, ten and Bridie, twelve. Being exempted from teaching needlework for a month would hardly have made a dent in Ann Connor's endless labour.

Because she was the oldest girl among so many brothers, it fell naturally to Bridie to be a second mother to the little ones and a second worker at the stove and the laundry copper. All the more so because Ann wasn't strong. Her cough had become part of who she was: a thin woman who, if you needed to find her, could always be tracked down by following the sound of that soft cough. And she was always tired. Bridie could see how her mother's strength was sucked out of her by the endless babies, another at the breast as soon as the last one was weaned.

It was Bridie who knew how to look after the yeast bottle now and it was her strong wrists that kneaded the loaves that sat rising under their tea towel every day, Bridie who riddled out the stove of a morning and chivvied one of the boys to fetch a handful of kindling from under the big gum tree, Bridie who milked the cow, churned the butter, Bridie who did the washing. Lifting a wet double bedsheet took as much strength as hoisting little Abigail onto your hip but gave you no smile in return. Alfred could sometimes be persuaded to help, but even Bridie's flattery of his strength was no consolation to him for the shame of doing women's work.

I'm having another look at the old photo and I can see, even in the blurry old print, how Ann is propping herself up, head bowed in the sun, as she holds the baby towards the camera. She'd married Joseph Connor when she was twenty-one. Then she'd had a baby more or less every two years.

So why would she want to be the needlework teacher as well? I thought perhaps it was a small gesture of independence, a bit of her own money, paltry though it was. But why was it her husband who applied for her leave?

The *Public Instruction Act 1880* explained:

> In schools containing female children but no female teacher, it will be the duty of the teacher's wife to teach needlework to the girls during at least four hours in each week. In forming an estimate of the efficiency of schools, the competency and usefulness of teachers' wives, and the time they devote to school duties, will be taken into account.

I'm imagining how it might have been when Connor got the teaching job. You'll be teaching the sewing, dear, he'd have told her. Oh no, my love, she'd have said. I won't do that. Laughed, not long married, and with only two children, still a young woman with a lovely fresh face, the cough not started, and the careless laugh of a person to whom life had not yet happened. He'd have had to explain: it was the regulation. He had a well-thumbed copy of the Act, a booklet every teacher was given so there could never be an excuse not to know the rules.

I remember sewing classes from my own primary school days. I managed eventually to produce a sad little sampler – a grubby bit of coarse pink cloth with a few not-very-straight lines of decorative stitches. But most of our time was spent on functional household items. This was the late 1950s but the things we learned to make were straight out of the nineteenth century. I'd never heard of pilchers, but we were supposed to knit a pair. I had no idea what a placket was, but we had to make a skirt that had one.

I know now that a placket was the way you did up a skirt before zips were invented. When I was being taught how to make one, the placket had been obsolete for nearly half a century, but in Ann Connor's time the laborious hand-sewing of it was an essential skill. Girls often produced a sampler of fancywork, but the real purpose of needlework in a household of modest means was nothing so dainty. It was about knowing how to make a dress, a shirt, a pair of trousers. How to mend and patch, how to turn sheets sides to middle to make them last longer. Now that schooling was compulsory, girls weren't at home learning those skills from their mothers, so the government was obliged to make sure they learned them at school.

In 1884 the going rate for a sewing teacher was a pound a month. When the sewing teacher was also the schoolteacher's wife, that pound was just added to her husband's salary. He was the person who was paid, so he was the person who applied when she needed leave.

Here's Joseph Connor, writing the pompous phases he's been told are the proper way to proceed. That word *accouchement* – what a fancy-pants word, he thinks. Obscuring, of course. Talk about a piece of furniture and talk about it in French, so as not to look at the thing itself. He's never been sure how to spell it, let alone say it. But the word *couch* is in there, and as he writes he sees a vivid image of a woman on a couch, legs apart, a baby being squeezed out. The cramped house beside the school at Currabubula doesn't run to a couch and he thinks of what will actually be happening soon, beyond that smarmy Frenchified word: his wife glimpsed through the doorway of the stuffy little bedroom, sitting on the edge of the bed, getting up, sitting down again, holding the brass bedstead, groaning. He'd never been present at the birth itself, that was between his wife and whatever woman was there with her, but there was no getting away from the sounds of a person in labour.

The look of this page in the file is extraordinary. Around and above and beside and on the back of Connor's few lines, there are marks made by a whole hierarchy of officials, each man (it would have been men) reading the document, running it through his mental catalogue of Departmental rules and regulations, and leaving his spoor to show he'd been there.

This particular page is stamped *20th March* by the Department of Public Instruction and given a number: *25173*. It's stamped again, *22nd March*, by the Chief Inspector's office and given another number:

35411. A handwritten *479* sits above that stamp. In the left-hand margin in red ink: *Submitted, 22.3.85*. Below that, also in red: *Approved on Schedule, 23.3.85*. Below that, a squiggle of initials and *25.3.85, Chief Inspector*. Below that, a big purple *A*, another squiggle, *26.3.85*, another stamp: *L C1 26 Sept*. Below that, *Letter written*, a squiggle, *28.3.85*. Below that, *Noted 10.10.85*. Along the bottom of the page: another squiggle, *12.10.85* and *Under-Secretary I concur, J.C.J.* Another set of initials, *G.H.*, and the number *18864*. Then *District Inspector: recommended, L.B. 13.10.85* and *Chief Inspector: I concur, J.D.B. 14.10.85*.

That's one reality: those men behind desks in Sydney with their stamps and pens busily working through their in-trays, their job to make a mark on the paper, while in remote Currabubula, in another reality altogether, Ann Connor leans hard against the kitchen table and calls to little Roland to run and fetch Mrs Fuller, because the baby's coming whether or not the Inspector gives permission.

10th June 1887

<u>Death certificate</u>
Date and place of death: 10 June 1887, Currabubula
Name and occupation: James Simon Connor
Sex and age: Male 4 1/6 years
Cause of death: Croup
Duration of last illness: 4 days
Medical attendant: Dr Atkins
When he last saw deceased: 8 June 1887

There's no time for Ann to mourn the child, because the new baby won't stop crying and Abigail's screaming for James, the two of them had been inseparable, and she seems to have forgotten how to use the potty and there are no clean nappies. Bridie's out in the yard boiling them up in the copper, and coughing. From the smoke, she says, but after a child's just coughed and wheezed his way to death, the sound fills the place with horror.

Efficiency and Usefulness

My grandmother apparently had her heart set on being a teacher, but when she asked her father if she could apply, he shouted, Over my dead body! It would shame him to have a daughter going out to work. People would think he couldn't support his family.

Grandma might have dodged a bullet. Nothing about being a pupil-teacher was easy, especially if you were female. Unless your family lived locally you had to find somewhere to board. A young man could board at the local hotel and have a few games of euchre in the evening without compromising his moral standing. But if you were a young woman, living at a hotel was out of the question. You'd have to find a respectable family to board with. Even so, a woman training for a profession was an oddity, regarded by many with disapproval and suspicion.

Apart from nursing, or being a nun if you were Catholic, teaching was the only real alternative to marriage that was open to a young woman in Currabubula at the end of the nineteenth century. If you could last through the three-year apprenticeship as a pupil-teacher, teaching did offer an alternative to waiting for Mr Right.

It was a slog, though. You worked in the schoolroom all day under the eye of the schoolmaster, teaching the little ones their letters. In a one-room school like Currabubula Public, the master would see and hear every mistake you made. After school you'd sit at the desk out the front with him beside you, going through *Sullivan's Arithmetic* or *Nelson's History of England* to prepare for the next exam. Even after that the day wasn't over because you had to do your night study, so that next afternoon you could show it to him.

Still, it was worth the hard work. Most people had to leave school when they turned fourteen because there were virtually no public high schools, but a pupil-teacher gained another three years of education. There was status in that. Plus you were paid, and there was a career path leading to a better salary as you went on.

It took about three years for a pupil-teacher to work through the exams that would qualify them to be in charge of a school on their own. But Mercy Stuckey left Currabubula at the end of Connor's first year, two years before her last exam. She was replaced by Euphemia Tierney.

6th October 1885
Teacher's Report on pupil-teacher Euphemia Tierney

Health: Miss Tierney appears to be in very fair health since her appointment to this school. She has not applied for leave of absence since her appointment.

Conduct out of school: Miss Tierney associates with none but respectable persons. I am of the opinion that her behaviour out of school and during her leisure time has been quite proper.

Conduct in school: I can find no fault with Miss Tierney's conduct in school, she has been punctual, diligent and obedient and she pays strict attention to her duty.

Diligence in home study: She works very hard indeed at her home lessons which she has always well prepared.

Progress since last examination: Since her appointment here her progress has been steady and continuous, and the result up to date is quite satisfactory.

Efficiency and usefulness: I examine Miss Tierney's class weekly and judging by its steady progress I conclude that she is both efficient and useful.

Has she received full instruction from her teacher? She has received full instruction in all the prescribed subjects and during the full time specified.

signed, J. Connor
Currabubula

In spite of this glowing report, less than a year later Euphemia Tierney also left. Elizabeth Short took her place.

25th October 1886
Teacher's Report on pupil-teacher Elizabeth Short

Health: Miss Short, so far as I can judge, does not suffer from any physical infirmity. She has every appearance of being a strong robust young woman. She has not since her appointment to this school applied for leave of absence, nor has she been absent from her duties at any time.

Conduct out of school: Miss Short's moral character is undoubtedly good; she associates with no one but those who are respectable, and her leisure time is usually occupied in reading good books.

Conduct in school: Punctuality: Good
Diligence: Very fair
Obedience: Excellent
Attention to duty: Very fair

Diligence in home study: She prepares her home lessons in a satisfactory manner.

Progress since last examination: Fair progress has been made by her during the three months she has been here.

Efficiency and usefulness: I regard both at present as "Tolerable" but as Miss Short is a painstaking young lady I anticipate an improvement in the near future.

Who teaches her needlework? Mrs Moorby, the lady with whom she boards.

Has she received full instruction from her teacher? She has received full instruction in the whole of the prescribed subjects during the full specified time.

signed, J. Connor

Just over a year later, something had happened to this *strong robust* young woman.

1st December 1887
Elizabeth Short to Joseph Connor

Sir, I beg to tender my resignation at the end of this month as pupil-teacher in this school. The cause of my tendering my resignation is that of failing health, which debars me from fulfilling my duties and prosecuting my studies in a satisfactory manner.

I have the honour etc.
Elizabeth Short

I can't help thinking that this is starting to look like a high turnover, and it makes me wonder what kind of master Joseph Connor was. He might have been kindly towards these young women – they were hardly older than his own daughter, after all, and his reports on them have a tone of working hard not to be critical. But I was curious enough to go back to the files and it turns out that Miss Stuckey and Miss Tierney didn't leave the profession – they just left Currabubula, finishing their training at other schools. Both of them went on to become teachers. Miss Short didn't – she resigned from the Service and married a few years later. She died in 1956 at the age of eighty-four. Her *failing health* seems to have made an excellent recovery.

Whatever caused this revolving door of pupil-teachers, Miss Short's resignation was remarkably convenient for Joseph Connor. The very same day she wrote her letter of resignation, he was taking advantage of it.

1st December 1887
Joseph Connor to Inspector Bucher

Sir,
I have the honour to apply for the temporary appointment of my daughter, Bridget Connor, to perform the duties of pupil-teacher in this school. She is an applicant for appointment as pupil-teacher, and is going up for examination I believe some day in this month, when I am confident she will succeed. Should she be temporarily appointed in the room of Miss Short, who is resigning at the end of this month, I will guarantee that she will perform the duties in a satisfactory manner until the result of her examination is made known, and without remuneration in case of her failure.

I have etc.
J. Connor

Bridie is thirteen or fourteen. I look again at the slim young woman in the long pale dress, standing at the end of the row of pupils, avoiding the eye of the camera. The young woman at the other end of the row, straining to stand at ramrod attention, is probably Miss Short, about to claim *failing health* and leave a space for Bridie to fill.

I've got a picture of Joseph Connor as a man proud of his daughter, a careful father doing what he can to ease her path. He'll steer her through the exams so that in a couple of years she'll have good marks in the finals and a string of glowing Teacher's Reports. With his help she'll be on her way to a privilege almost unknown for a woman in 1887: money of her own and something resembling a career. Bridie would have a much easier time as a pupil-teacher than Miss Stuckey, Miss Tierney or Miss Short. She'd be living at home, with the support of family around her. Her father had trained her in what was expected and always ridden her hard to do well in class, so she was already used to learning great slabs of knowledge off by heart, had been drilled in the finer points of apostrophes and compound interest till she could do them in her sleep.

From as early as she could remember, Bridie's known what's ahead of her: helping her mother in the house, of course, but also training to be a teacher. Her father has explained time after time the advantages of having a profession. He doesn't ask whether she wants that. She's only a child. She doesn't expect to be asked.

And she's a girl. It's taken for granted that men make every important decision. But by the time she's studying for the exam to become a pupil-teacher, she understands more about how things work. Teaching brings advantages, yes, but a woman's career will always be limited. Female pupil-teachers and female teachers are only paid half the male rate, because it's assumed they'll never be the breadwinner. A woman will only ever be put in charge of a small school, or be assistant to a man at a bigger one. The Department tends to assign female teachers to hard-to-staff schools because women have so few employment choices.

She watches her friends leave school the day they turn fourteen. They'll stay at home helping their mothers and embroidering table-cloths for their glory boxes. Then after a few years they'll get married. She thinks she probably will too, eventually – it seems a woman's inevitable future. Becoming a pupil-teacher is really just a superior version of what her schoolmates are doing, marking time until they marry. As a teacher, your education might let you make a better marriage, that's all. Oh, you might even marry a doctor or a lawyer! Once you married, you probably wouldn't continue teaching. Women were supposed to put their families first, so you had to ask the Department for permission to stay in the Service after you married. It was only likely to be granted if there were no men who wanted the job.

She's the different one, the one staying on at school. Does she want to be a teacher? To stand, the way she watches her father do every day, dinning the times tables and the Rivers of Africa into a roomful of children who couldn't care less? That's a question she tries not to ask herself.

I'm peering at the old photo again. There's a sense of her turning away, of disengaging, of not wanting to be part of what's going on. That makes me think she might not have been enthusiastic about what she was being funnelled into. Might she felt the way I would have in that situation: outrage at the injustice of it, that her life was so entirely constrained by men, and limited to such narrow and badly paid paths?

In any case, whether or not she wants to train as a teacher, it turns out she'll have to wait.

2nd December 1887

Inspector Bucher to District Inspector Miller

There is no eligible applicant pupil-teacher nearer than Tamworth, but four applicants at Currabubula are awaiting examination, and it is very probable that one or two of the number will pass.

The authorisation of the temporary employment of the teacher's daughter would, I think, give her an unfair claim to appointment, to the prejudice of the others now awaiting examination at Currabubula.

I recommend that the teacher be informed that the Department is not prepared to temporarily employ any person who has not passed the necessary preliminary examination, that consequently his application for the temporary employment of his daughter is refused.

Matthew Bucher

Three other applicants in Currabubula! That seems a lot for such a small place. Joseph Connor's was the only school, so unless some of them had private tutors they must all have been his students. He'd have known them well. And yet he's going to try to sneak his daughter in ahead of them. An *unfair claim* is exactly what he wants.

He curses the fact that Inspector Jones has been assigned to another district. Jones would have found a loophole, waved Bridie through. But Connor had met Matthew Bucher, the new man, knew that he was a different sort of fellow. A damn teetotaller! There'd be no sitting with Bucher over a beer at the Albion.

In May 1888, Daniel Withers was appointed to the position. He was the fourth pupil-teacher in four years.

A Number of Dead Mice

23rd May 1888
Joseph Connor to Inspector Bucher

Sir, I have the honour to inform you that the water in the school underground tank has become unfit for consumption; it smells and tastes badly, and I am of opinion that, besides the accumulation of sediment for the past six years, it contains a number of dead mice.

I have etc.
J. Connor

When our children were young, my husband and I lived in a decrepit house in an old Sydney suburb. At one point we had some plumbing work done that gradually expanded from a small job into one that involved digging up the whole backyard to a depth of several metres. As they dug deeper and deeper, the men uncovered a huge spooky brick-lined chamber with a narrow top. An underground water tank, the plumber told us. Rainwater from the roof would have been fed into it and pumped out manually. There was something horrible about unknowingly having had this dark nasty dungeon under us when we'd sung "Happy Birthday" on the back deck and given the baby her first taste of ice-cream.

So I can see the tank Connor is talking about. Can imagine the water: dank, stagnant, lying there cold and still. And the place where the water came in: a pipe from the gutter and a collar of galvanised iron to keep things from falling in. Except the collar has rusted. The line where the solder runs has failed and made a gap, and some poor mouse has thought to slake its thirst.

26th May 1888
Inspector Bucher to Joseph Connor

Mr Connor, obtain & attach hereto one or two tenders for the work.

Matthew Bucher

1st June 1888
Joseph Connor to Inspector Bucher

Mr Bucher, attached are two tenders for the work. I have asked three others to tender for the work but they do not appear to care about doing so.

J. Connor

Now this is odd – they *do not appear to care about doing so*. They're not just refusing, they're making a performance of it. They're not even bothering to pretend regret, or come up with an excuse.

So, here's Joseph Connor, going one afternoon to William Johnson's house, knocking on the door. He can smell the tea cooking, mutton chops and potato, and he can hear the wife calling to the squabbling children. Johnson comes to the door, a man he knows – his children are Connor's pupils. Johnson's face falls when he sees Connor. He doesn't ask him in.

So Connor smiles, laying himself out to charm this churl. The water, the mouse, the failed metal collar. Johnson watches him as he speaks, like a deaf man reading lips. There's no expression on his face. Even a little jest about the mouse gets nothing but that stony look. Connor reminds him that his children are drinking the water too. And that makes Johnson speak for the first time. Bring their own bottles from home, he says. Don't never drink the school water.

Then you'll not be interested in doing the cleaning of it, Connor says. Johnson's shaking his head before Connor has finished the sentence, closing the door a few seconds faster than is polite.

He's got them offside somehow, but if he knows why, he's not sharing that with the Inspector. I wonder if he feels as if he's one of the top lot in this little society. *They do not appear to care* – it's a haughty tone, like gentry complaining about the servants. A man like Johnson could resent him for his relative wealth and status, and that tone. But Johnson and the others are working men. They'd surely be glad of the job, no matter their resentment. Maybe Connor's just the kind of person who rubs people up the wrong way, not understanding the minuet of conversation, the giving and taking, the advancing and retreating, the real conversation going under the surface of some banal exchange.

2nd June 1888
Inspector Bucher to Joseph Connor

Mr Connor, the prices asked are exorbitant. Try if you cannot obtain some reasonable tender.

Matthew Bucher

4th June 1888

Joseph Connor to Inspector Bucher

Mr Bucher, attached are two fresh tenders. Took stone off top of tank and saw some dead mice in putrid state. Lindley is one of those I at first asked for a tender. On examining the pump today I find top of rod and bolt both nearly worn through and sucker almost useless. As Lindley is a blacksmith he says he is making no extra charge for repairing the pump. Five and a half feet of water in tank.

J. Connor

When I went to Currabubula School on my first research trip for the book about my mother, I noticed an old-fashioned pump handle near the gate. It's stuck in the concrete pavement and painted pale green. On that long-ago sunny day it meant nothing in particular to me, but I photographed it anyway.

I dig out the photo and look at it again. Now that I've read the file, the pump handle isn't just a meaningless Ye Olde thing in the playground along with Ye Olde school bell and Ye Olde boot scraper. It's Mrs Connor heaving away, pulling the handle up and down and watching the water squirt – slowly, too slowly – into the bucket underneath while she tries not to lose her temper with the way Abigail's grizzling, hanging onto her leg and dragging at her arm. She wants to let the handle flop down, walk away, leave the whole silly thing, but there's no other way to get water to wash the nappies and she's just put the last clean one on Adolphus.

Or Joseph has made it another of his routine jobs: to go out in the morning and heave away at the pump, filling the barrel in the kitchen and the other one at the corner of the schoolhouse. His big hand around that bit of now-pale-green metal, cursing the slowness of it, the relentlessness of thirst.

5th June 1888
Inspector Bucher to Joseph Connor

Mr Connor, can you not get the work done at a more reasonable cost – say 3 pounds?

Matthew Bucher

7th June 1888
Joseph Connor to Inspector Bucher

Mr Bucher, attached are two fresh tenders.

J. Connor

7th June 1888
Inspector Bucher to District Inspector Miller

I recommend that the teacher be authorised to have the school pump repaired and the underground tank emptied & cleaned at a cost not exceeding 3 pounds ten shillings.

The stated price is rather high but is little more than one third of that asked in the two tenders first forwarded by the teacher.

M. Bucher

In the end, finding someone to do the work and negotiating the price and getting the tank cleaned out took nearly two months. Then there'd have to be rain to fill it up again. In the meantime, what did the Connors drink? Water from the creek, I suppose, carried up in barrels on the dray.

Poor old Connor was not only wrangling up to seventy kids in a crammed classroom, and his own kids in an equally crammed little house, he also had to haggle with local men and justify the expenditure of three pounds ten shillings to his bosses, and for a couple of months he had to lug water up from the creek for his pupils and his family.

For heaven's sake, Bucher, I'm thinking, go easy on the poor man. Just say yes, so the Connors don't have to go on drinking water with dead mice floating in it!

Accouchement

3rd September 1888
Joseph Connor to Inspector Bucher

Sir, I have the honour to apply for leave of absence for Mrs Connor during one month from this date, from her duties as teacher of needlework in this school in consequence of her accouchement.

I have etc.
J. Connor
Teacher

This child was Louis. He's Ann Connor's eighth *accouchement*. Adolphus was about eighteen months old. Probably two children in nappies, then.

Have Much Pleasure

21st August 1888
<u>Teacher's Report on pupil-teacher on probation Daniel Withers, age 16.</u>

<u>Health</u>: His health is good, no symptoms of illness were noticeable since his appointment on probation. He has had no leave of absence since his appointment.

<u>Conduct out of school</u>: His moral character so far as I could observe has been blameless. He does not associate with anyone of doubtful character, and his leisure time is usually spent in the company of the members of his own family.

<u>Conduct in school</u>: Punctuality: He is fairly punctual
Diligence: He is fairly diligent
Obedience: He is perfectly obedient
Attention to duty: He pays due attention to his duties.

<u>Diligence in home study</u>: He prosecutes his home studies with a reasonable amount of diligence.

<u>Progress since last examination</u>: He has not yet been examined since his appointment.

Efficiency and usefulness: He has made a satisfactory progression in this respect since his appointment. He is very willing to do what he can.

Has he received full instruction? He has received full instruction in all prescribed subjects and for the full time specified.

signed, J. Connor
Currabubula

There's something perfunctory about this report compared with the earlier ones, and the tone is cooler. Does that mean something, or was Joseph Connor just in a hurry that day?

17th December 1888
Daniel Withers to Joseph Connor

Sir,
I regret to have to inform you that I am too ill to attend the examination to which I have been cited to attend this day at Tamworth. I have the honour to enclose the certificate of a medical man in confirmation as to what I state of my illness.

I have etc.
D. Withers

15th December 1888
Tamworth

Mr D. Withers has been suffering from Bilious Vomiting and Diarrhoea for two days past and is still evidently far from well.

Thos. B. Crisp FRCSC

17th December 1888
Daniel Withers to Joseph Connor

Sir,
I beg to request that leave of absence be granted me from the 17 to the 20th instant inclusive as I am too ill to perform my duties. I have already given you Sir the certificate of a medical man as to the nature of my illness.

I have the honour etc.
D. Withers

18th December 1888
Joseph Connor to the Chief Inspector

To the Chief Inspector: I have much pleasure in recommending that Mr Wither's request be granted, as he is evidently too weak to perform his duties.

J. Connor

I can't let myself think the worst, but there's no avoiding the fact that this is uncannily convenient for Connor. If Withers had been able to sit for the exam in December and passed, he'd have been no longer on probation but a certified pupil-teacher. In the ordinary way of things, he'd have stayed at Currabubula for the next three years. Bridie would have had to apply to be pupil-teacher at another school. Tamworth or Werris Creek were the closest, and they were too far to travel to every day, so Connor would have had to pay for her board. Plus she'd have been at the mercy of the teacher there, rather than under his own helping hand.

I suppose it's my twenty-first-century ear, but *I have much pleasure* strikes a sour note. Daniel Withers is a young man of sixteen, in good health in August but so sick in December that he's too weak to work or to sit for a vital exam. Even allowing for the routinely elaborate language of nineteenth-century official letters, it's an oddly cheerful form of words. I picture Connor carefully shaping the letters and laughing aloud at the way the bureaucratic formula is, for once, absolutely spot on.

22nd February 1889

Currabubula Public School: Bridget Connor appointed as pupil-teacher on probation. Examined January 1888, 731 marks. Present age 14 1/2 years. Teacher's daughter.

In his own punctilious, goody-two-shoes way, Joseph Connor was as persistent as a cat.

1st June 1889
<u>Teacher's Report on Bridget Connor, pupil-teacher</u>

Miss Connor is not suffering from any physical infirmity; I have not noticed any symptoms of failure in health since her appointment. No leave of absence has been granted since her appointment on probation to this school.

Her conduct out of school is irreproachable; she associates with none but the members of her own family.

She is punctual, diligent, obedient, and she pays strict attention to her duties.

All her home lessons are prepared with diligence and despatch.

She has made good progress since her appointment on probation.

She performs her duties efficiently, having effected a great improvement in her class since taking charge of it; she is certainly very useful in this school.

Joseph Connor, Teacher

In this cascade of praise, the one thing Joseph Connor doesn't mention is that Bridget Connor is his daughter. Not that he's concealing the fact, of course – it's on record. But he's not going to bring it to anyone's attention.

She's associating with *none but the members of her own family*. Was there really no skiving off with a gang of friends to the creek, craybobbing with a bit of old bacon the way my mother did during her time in Currabubula? No dances at Newland's Hall, with the local paper praising the refreshments and describing everyone's frocks?

As his daughter and pupil, Bridie had been with her father every day and night of her life. Now, at fourteen, she was going to be with him every day and every night for another three years as his pupil-teacher. When Connor writes that she associates only with the members of her own family, that might just be pious rhetoric for the form. But if it was literally true, wouldn't it have been desperately claustrophobic?

Those Cess-Pits

26th January 1890
Telegram to Mr J. Connor, Public School, Currabubula

Child has diphtheria fear chance of recovery slight.

Thos. B. Crisp, Tamworth

Until recently, diphtheria had been virtually eradicated in Australia, thanks to vaccines. But before the 1930s, whole families of children died of it. It's an infection that makes a membrane grow over the throat so the victim slowly suffocates. Until the 1920s there was no cure. It's extremely contagious and has a high death rate among children.

27th January 1890
Joseph Connor to Inspector Bucher

Sir,
I regret having to inform you that diphtheria has broken out in my family. My wife took one of my children to Dr Crisp in Tamworth this morning, and the doctor informed me by telegram (which I herewith append) that the child is suffering from diphtheria, with but a slight chance of his recovery. Two others of my children

have suspicious symptoms, but the doctor has not seen them yet. A neighbour's child died of diphtheria on the 23rd inst.

I would suggest that the school be closed from the 28th inst to the 15th Feb inclusive.

I have the honour to be, Sir, your humble servant
J. Connor, Teacher

Of course it wouldn't have been appropriate for Joseph Connor to reveal in an official letter how he felt about one of his children having a life-threatening disease and two others probably having it too. He's speaking of it in the same cool phrases he might use to report a broken window. *I regret having to inform you.*

The feelings are there, though, buried in that word *regret*. It's part of a formula but at an unconscious level, surely *I regret having to inform you* stands in for *I am racked with grief, panic, distress, despair*.

And that elegant little construction, *with but a slight chance of his recovery* – I see him at the desk in the empty schoolroom, the children gone home for the day but who knows how many already infected. He can hear his own children coughing in the house. He dips his pen in the ink to put the nightmare into words. Was it some small comfort, on a day with no comfort, to shape the sentence into something tight and neat and controlled, a phrase that could be a line from a poem, when what was happening around him was so ugly and spiralling away beyond any human agency?

My wife took one of my children to the doctor – that was a couple of hours in the buggy, Currabubula to Tamworth, in the January heat. When Ann got there, she'd have gone to the doctor's house, probably one of the biggest and grandest in Tamworth. Taking a child to the doctor was a big deal, and a mark of how gravely sick he or she was.

I have a sense of it from my own childhood, the respect and awe in which Doctor was held. Dr Bligh was a big sombre man with thick iron-grey hair and very pinkly clean fingers. On the rare occasions that he paid a house call there was a sense of royalty visiting. My mother would bustle about changing sheets, putting me in new pyjamas, bringing a basin in to where I lay in bed, wiping my face and washing my hands before he arrived. Seeing my mother's awe of Dr Bligh made me frightened of him, and when he did that missing-thumb trick that awkward men do with children to amuse them, I burst into tears.

Ann Connor would have known that Dr Crisp couldn't do much. He'd have gone through the motions: looked down the child's throat, listened with the stethoscope. He might have told Mrs Connor to get the child to breathe steam with eucalyptus oil, or written a script for a concoction to gargle. But he and Mrs Connor – the child too, probably – would have known there was no real treatment. All you had was luck and hope.

Then it was back to Currabubula in the buggy, the child now too limp to cough, the breath coming in strange squeaks through an almost-closed throat.

27th January 1890

Inspector Bucher to District Inspector Miller

A pupil of this school died on Friday last from Diphtheria, and the teacher's child is ill.

I have instructed the teacher to close school pending receipt of further instructions and to forward one or two tenders for emptying the WCs.

M. Bucher

I wondered why Matthew Bucher was choosing this moment to worry about emptying the WCs, but it turns out that he was just following the conventional science of the day. People thought diphtheria spread from smelly air.

The school had three toilets: one for boys, one for girls, and one for the teacher's family. They weren't actually toilets as such. They were long-drops, pits in the ground topped with a plank with a bottom-sized hole in it. When they're used by a lot of people, long-drops fill up. They smell and bring the flies. Eventually they have to be emptied.

28th January 1890
Joseph Connor to Inspector Bucher

Sir,
I do not deem it advisable, Sir, to give an estimate of the cost of emptying these cess-pits, as, by experience, I find that when people are asked what they would charge for such a job, they name a price far too high, and, if the teacher does not assist them in obtaining that price, they take a very strong dislike to him.

I am under the impression, Sir, that the better plan would be to authorise me to call for tenders, which I could forward to you instead of the usual estimate.

I have also the honour to apply for a box of disinfectant.

I have etc.
J. Connor

There was no need for me to be complicated in my wonderings about why Connor got on the wrong side of people. Here it is, laid out clearly, and it's as simple as money. The people in Currabubula have watched the Department build a brick schoolhouse and a substantial cottage next to it for the teacher's family. They know the teacher is well paid. Their children use slates and books provided free of charge by the Department, not to mention the toilets and the drinking water and the dunny-cleaning. It's natural for parents to think that the Department is a bottomless well of money. But they've learned that whenever the teacher – the Department's representative in Currabubula – needs a job done, he cries poor. Connor knows how different things are, how hard it is to get money out of the tight Departmental purse. But there's no way for him to explain that.

What's happening in Currabubula isn't about what sort of a man Joseph Connor is. It's about what happens to a man caught between a penny-pinching government and the expectations of the locals.

A very strong dislike. He'd tell himself it wasn't personal. Still, it would hurt.

10th February 1890
Joseph Connor to Inspector Bucher

Sir,
It was not until today that I succeeded in getting anyone who would be willing to clean out the closets but the sum of 20 pounds which this man wants for doing the work appears to me to be so large that I cannot consider myself justified in employing him for that amount without further instructions. I am under the impression that, were I authorised to offer 15 pounds, the work would be done for it.

Dr Crisp attended my children on the 8th inst and he pronounces them out of danger.

The same disease is spreading rapidly amongst the children who have been attending this school, as many as fifteen of them being at present under medical treatment.

J. Connor

Connor has to spell out that he knows the price is too high. Otherwise the Inspector might think he's in cahoots with the men doing the tendering. But they've arrived at a bit of a deadlock and at this point Matthew Bucher must have had a bright idea: the best way to arrive at a fair price for emptying the pits would be to measure the amount of material in them. Bucher's letter isn't in the file, but Joseph Connor's reply is.

12th February 1890
Joseph Connor to Inspector Bucher

Sir,
There may be 60 cubic feet in the cesspits but of course this is only conjecture, for, as they extend underground, there can be no actual measurement.

Yours respectfully
J. Connor

Given how silly Bucher's suggestion is, Connor's response is remarkably restrained. I wonder how many drafts it took to erase any whiff of what he really thought.

But actually it's not quite erased. Most of his other letters end with an abbreviation of the formula *I have the honour to be, Sir, your humble and obedient servant*, the conventional sign-off in an official letter from an underling to a superior. This is one of the few times he writes *Yours respectfully* instead. Yet *respectful* is surely the last thing he'd have been feeling towards someone who expected him to measure the contents of the long-drops. The word *respect* makes you think straight away of its opposite. Unallowable feelings of scorn, contempt and frustration fume up from the word whose ostensible purpose is to smother them. In all the many drafts I imagine him writing, this might have been the way he finally found to deliver the bitter sarcasm that matched his feelings.

15th February 1890
Inspector Bucher to District Inspector Miller

The teacher states that there may be 60 cubic feet of soil in the pits. As there are two school closets & one private one which have been in use for years, his estimate is ridiculously low. Probably there are quite 300 feet of soil etc.

M. Bucher

I'm starting to dislike Matthew Bucher. First he wants Connor to do something silly. When Connor obediently makes a cautious attempt, Bucher throws him under the bus. His own estimate seems presumptuous. The fact is, it was anyone's guess how much shit was in those holes.

25th February 1890
Joseph Connor to the Under-Secretary, Department of Public Instruction

Sir, in reply to your telegram dated 24th inst re cleaning of cess-pits, I have the honour to state that Messrs Oldham and Anderson have completed the work in a satisfactory manner.

I now have the honour to apply for a box of disinfectant for this School.

I have etc.
J. Connor

A *box of disinfectant* was just powdered lime. It would have cost about twopence.

28th February 1890
District Inspector Miller to Inspector Bucher

In what respect is this an urgent matter? Disinfectant should not be needed if the teacher sees that the WCs are kept clean.

W.M. Miller, District Inspector

Joseph Connor is the only one here who's calling the toilets what they are: cesspits. The men from the Department – Inspector Bucher, and now Bucher's boss, District Inspector Miller – are calling them WCs, as if they're nice white ceramic water closets full of lovely clean water. Inspector Bucher lived in Tamworth, so his own toilet might have been an actual water closet. The toilets of the officials in Sydney probably were, too. They might never have known what it was like to sit over a smelly hole in the ground.

None of those Department men wants to deal with the reality of bodies and their sordid discharges, and this insistence on the need for a box of disinfectant is forcing them to think about what's behind the screen of polite words. It's making everyone snippy. The air is fizzing with the sound of men asserting themselves.

Over the last two months the issue of the Currabubula dunnies has gone up the ranks of the Department, from the local Inspector to the District Inspector, arriving right at the top of the tree, the desk of the Under-Secretary of the Department. Matthew Bucher would have wanted to choose his words carefully. I imagine him dipping his pen in the ink and pausing, trying to find a way to convince his masters while at the same time not drawing too vivid a picture.

2nd March 1890
Inspector Bucher to the Chief Inspector

Sir,
It is my experience that whenever WCs are emptied, more or less of the refuse sticks to the walls, and renders the use of disinfectant imperative.
Hence my recommendation in this case.

M. Bucher

At this point I feel nothing but sympathy for Joseph Connor. He's a man beset from all sides, disliked by at least some of the townsfolk and distrusted by his employer. He made more money than most of the men in Currabubula, but he earned every penny.

The little shadow of doubt over the matter of not *learning* Lizzie Woodbridge and stealing the children's lunches has gone. I'm dismissing as ridiculous the suspicion that he got rid of all those pupil-teachers to make way for his daughter. And I've explained to my own satisfaction why people in the town don't like him. I feel for him, and I'm glad to know that none of his children ended up dying of diphtheria.

Accouchement

17th November 1890
Joseph Connor to Inspector Elliott

Sir,
I have the honour to apply for the exemption of my wife from teaching needlework for one calendar month from the above date in consideration of her accouchement.

I have etc.
J. Connor

This child is Beatrice. Ann Connor is now forty years old and this is the tenth time she's been through an *accouchement.* She's been pregnant or breastfeeding since her marriage. Was there no way off this runaway horse of family?

Catholics though they were, I think they might have tried. Even the devout have been known to, and there was no prying priest in little Currabubula. Without having ever spoken about it, they might have had no great objection to preventing what God made the act for. Joseph tries the business of pulling out, but oh, that's a tricky bit of timing. Ann tries the rigmarole of the douche straight after but that doesn't do the job either. Unbeknown to her husband, she's even tried the Housewife's Friend, big brown suppositories bought under the counter in the anonymity of Sydney by her good-hearted sister and mailed to her.

But Nature is more more cunning than Man, or God more determined. And Joseph in the dark watches of the night asks himself what a man was to do with his needs. The priests did it, resisted the cravings of the flesh. It would be a kindness to the other party to do without. That he knows. Once she'd laughed and whispered, but not now. She's silent, perhaps asleep, perhaps counting the minutes. His need now is something that lies between them, a thing that rules them but that they have no words to talk about.

Rancorous Intermeddler

The forged letters had arrived in 1885 and for five years after that there were no more complaints about Connor, just those odd difficulties and resistances. Now, out of nowhere, there's another complaint.

> **7th August 1890**
> From A.W. Brown to J.H. Carruthers, Minister for Public Education
>
> Sir – I beg to bring under your notice the following grievances.
>
> 1. That, the piece of land which is fenced off from the children's play ground which belongs to the Currabubula Public School, is used as cattle yard.
> 2. That, a number of cattle in this neighbourhood are suffering from a disease.
> 3. That, a pigsty is erected inside of the fence of the children's play ground, within a few yards of the girls' closet.
> 4. That, a cart shed is erected on the same.
>
> What with the late rains and the cattle constantly tramping upon this yard, above now presents a disgraceful and shocking appearance.

I have the honour to be, Sir, your most obedient and humble servant,
A.W. Brown

P.S. if you can help it do not let my name become public, as I do not want to cause ill-feeling.
A.W. Brown

Cow poop, pig poop, mud: it's an awful picture of the schoolyard. I can smell the stink, feel the mud heavy on my boots, see the depressing dirty muddle and clutter.

But this is the kind of problem you'd work out without recourse to the Minister, surely? You'd have a word with Connor. You'd try to make it a bit jokey.

Maybe A.W. Brown tried that and it didn't work. That can happen. You bump into your neighbour in the street: Oh, hi, Anne, just wanted to have a word ... It might be about the noisy air conditioner. Or the dog barking. Or the vine climbing over the roof. You keep it light. You offer to pay for the motor to be moved, offer to walk the dog, offer to go halves on the vine-trimming. But even before you finish the first sentence it's all gone wrong. Anne bristles up, says something about your loud music or your trespassing cat. Then you get on your high horse too and suddenly out of nowhere you're having a barney.

I went looking for A.W. Brown. He was Arthur Brown, a local farmer, twenty-two years old. He lived with his father, also named Arthur Brown. *Do not let my name become public*. You could say that's reasonable. Currabubula was a small place and no one likes a dobber. But that little postscript makes me think of those forgeries – nastiness hurled from a safe hiding place. I'm wondering if A.W. Brown might be *The Voice of the People*.

He might be, but he's not the only person who has a bone to pick with Joseph Connor.

10th August 1890
John Bradbury to the Minister for Public Instruction

Sir,
Permit me Sir to give a few facts in regard to complaint by Mr Brown he was Correct In the Playground being used as a Stockyard I have seen a dead beast on it and it was Skined thear I beg to inform you a number of cattle in this neighbourhood are suffering from a dease. Considering how dangerous the flies are when such Beasts allowed to live, it will be wiser to rid the yard of all catle. If he want to dary farm have we to bare the Consequences of Diphtheria and other throat deases no doubt you are awar in the Past year the school been Closed on account of dipthearia Sir a Change of master would be of great benefit to the Place. I send five children

Yours respectfully
John Bradbury

The lack of punctuation makes it difficult to follow. The odd spelling is distracting. The muddle of random thoughts one after the other is confusing. Still, the thought of children playing in that yard is disturbing.

14th August 1890
Joseph Connor to Inspector Elliott

Sir, I regret exceedingly that I should be the cause (however unintentionally), of giving the Minister and officers of the Department so much trouble.

In reply to the charges of Messrs Brown and Bradbury, it is quite true that part of the playground is fenced off and used as a milking yard for about 6 cows, and the calves are kept there at night.

I have put cows and calves in the playground after school hours, in order to eat down the long grass, which would conceal vermin and snakes, and on dewy mornings wet the children to the waist.

The statement that some cattle in the vicinity are suffering from a disease is a deliberate falsehood. Some two years ago a calf of mine became inflated from eating trefoil which then grew abundantly on the playground. This is the instance I presume which is referred to. I was quite aware of the danger to which I exposed this calf, but I was anxious to get the trefoil eaten down. The calf died from the cause I have stated, and of course I had him instantly removed.

There was a pig sty about 30 yards from the girls' WC. The sty had a boarded floor and was kept quite clean. It has recently been pulled down and removed.

As regards the cleanliness of the playground, I will venture to affirm that there is not a cleaner in the colony.

The cart-shed is erected where complained of. No person in Currabubula carts wood for hire. In order to provide firewood for my own private use as well as for the school I was compelled to buy a horse and cart and draw the fuel in myself. The shed is erected on the playground as there is no entrance for a dray to my private yard.

I have been teacher of this school for upwards of 6 years, and have been frequently informed by different persons that Mr Brown bears me a strong sectarian animosity. I believe that his aim in bringing forward this charge is because of religious differences and not from any regard for the welfare of the school. I have been informed on good authority that he is determined to do me an injury if he can.

> As regards the antecedents of Mr Brown, and the purity or otherwise of his motives, it may not be out of place for me to inform you, Sir, that he has been brought to trial for shooting his brother dead some eight or nine years ago, and acquitted I am informed for want of sufficient evidence.
>
> I am, Sir, yours respectfully,
> J. Connor, Teacher

There's that suck-up tone again: *regret exceedingly that I should be the cause of giving the Minister so much trouble.* Inspector Bucher has moved on and Archibald Elliott is the new man Connor has to deal with. Connor's still feeling his way with Elliott. He hopes this tone will get him on side – lining Connor up with the Minister and his *officers*, the professionals dealing together with a hazard of the profession. *Oh, what a nuisance these complaints are, aren't they?*

He begins by answering the accusations in an airy, I'm-not-bothered way, but then the cool mask slips and he goes on the offensive. The business about the dead calf isn't an error, not even just a *falsehood.* It's a *deliberate falsehood.* Not a mistake: malice.

And where does this business of *sectarian animosity* suddenly come from? I can well believe religious difference could be a problem in Currabubula in 1890, although no hint of it has appeared since the brief mention in the forged letter five years earlier. But the thing about this accusation is that the person bringing it up isn't A.W. Brown or John Bradbury. It's Joseph Connor, making a vague claim based on being *frequently informed by different persons*. And you can see why he wants to haul it in: it's a distraction. Suddenly it's in the room, a great hairy elephant, making everyone look at *sectarian animosity* rather than *cattle and pigs*.

What a glimpse this letter gives into the laborious life of Currabubula in the 1890s. Poor Connor was not only the teacher of sixty or seventy children. He and his wife also had to organise six milking cows – that meant bringing them in from wherever they were grazing, milking them and taking them out again, twice a day, every day. The calves had to be brought in at night and taken back in the morning. He had to harness up the horse – also kept in a paddock somewhere, needing to be caught and brought in – and trundle off in the dray to get firewood, not just for his own household's cooking and heating, but in winter for the school as well. He'd have to split the wood and stack it and bring armloads inside every day. His life, the sheer hard physical work of it, wasn't that different from the poorest of his neighbours. Joseph Connor was the teacher, but he was also something like the janitor.

As for the business about Brown shooting his brother dead – oh, what juicy stuff, a vivid thread of dark and dirt! Straight away a picture springs to mind. Violent rednecks out for trouble in a house full of guns and alcohol.

I went looking, and it's true: in 1882 Arthur Brown did shoot dead Edward Brown. Arthur was thirteen. Edward was his half-brother, older by ten years.

29th July 1882
Australian Town & Country Journal

The coroner held an inquest at Tamworth yesterday on the body of a boy, named Edward Henry Brown, who was shot by his brother at Currabubula last Saturday. Evidence was given by the medical officer, the police and several railway labourers who witnessed the affair, and it was then adjourned till Wednesday.

> The inquest was concluded late last evening, when the jury returned a verdict that the deceased came by his death by a gunshot wound inflicted by his brother, Arthur Brown, but there was no evidence to show whether or not accidentally.

Knowing a bit more has the effect of sobering my glee at that oh-so-attractively movie-ready scenario. Yes, it's easy to visualise Arthur Brown taking aim at his half-brother. Young Arthur might have pulled the trigger in rage, hatred, jealousy. But it's also not hard to imagine an accident. There are plenty of guns in the country, and always death waiting to happen when a couple of boys go out rabbitting. That's more interesting and perhaps more true than the stereotype. That's a story about something unconscious welling up and making the gun go off at just the wrong moment in just the wrong direction, without intention but bursting with smothered meanings.

That story wouldn't be about the violent moment, exciting though that would be to write or read, but what came after: guilt, grief, regret. A boy of thirteen marked for life. *Oh, there's Arthur Brown, he shot his brother dead.* It would be the story of a boy growing into a man who had to get up every day and sit across the kitchen table from his father, whose firstborn he'd shot and killed on some awful day of chaos and blood.

But Connor planted the picture of the house full of crude violence, and my imagination has obediently made it seem real. Why has he done that? It's like *sectarian animosity*. Suddenly we're not looking at Joseph Connor. We're looking at Arthur Brown with a gun in his hand.

23 August 1890
Inspector Elliott to the Chief Inspector

Sir,
I have visited the Currabubula Public School and beg to report:

1. On the occasion of my visit, the yard was quite dry.
2. The pigsty and cart shed are erected on a portion of the playground not frequented by the children. The sty when I saw it was unused, quite dry and clean, and in no way objectionable.

I recommend that Mr Brown and Mr Bradbury be informed that "the Inspector for the district has visited the Currabubula PS and sees nothing in the use made of the premises by the teacher likely to interfere with the health and comfort of the pupils. The Minister is therefore of opinion that it is unnecessary to take any action in the matter."

A. Elliott

Inspector Elliott seems a little perfunctory here in dealing with the matter of the cattle on the playground, and there's also a bit of slippage about the pigsty. Inspector Elliott describes it as *unused*. Joseph Connor says it has been *pulled down and removed*.

A word in your ear, Connor, I hear Elliott murmuring as the two men stand at the side of the playground looking at the various structures, flapping away an early fly or two, the long shadows of the morning lying in stripes along the rough grass. Might be an idea to get rid of that sty, eh? Elliott says. Consider it done, sir, Connor replies.

9th September 1890
A.W. Brown to the Minister for Public Instruction

Dear Sir,
I am in receipt of yours dated 29th inst in reply to my letter re the PS "premises" at Currabubula, and am sorry to think my complaint has been treated so lightly. I am conscious of the "Inspector's" visit, and to my personal knowledge the morning he inspected the premises, there was no less than five (5) head of cattle, on the play ground, which is only part of the stock constantly to be found there, also the "Pigsty" which is not allowed in any municipality, within a reasonable distance of any street or thoroughfare.

Of course if you decide that this is a state of thing that should not be taken notice of, am inclined to think the sanitary "condition" of our "Public Instructions" are not in a healthy condition – and soliciting your further investigation when I am prepared to meet your "Inspector" and bring evidence to substantiate my report.

I deny that I have ever mentioned to any person that Mr Connor and I have had religious differences. It is a deliberate lie on the part of Mr Connor's informant.

You say it is unnecessary to interfere so long as it remains in its present creditable condition. Sir, I must differ from you because from practical experiences I find it is very unclean and unhealthy to have Cattle enclosed within a yard near the house where we live, and no matter how often the manure is clean up you cannot get rid of the nauseous and injurious smells.

In conclusion may state it not with any desire to injure the "Teacher" that I have brought this matter under your notice. but purely for the sake of the health & comfort of the children attending the school and through constant complaints made by the parents of the children, some of whom are also willing to come before you or your "Inspector" in support of this complaint.

I have the honour to be, sir, your most obedient and humble servant,

A.W. Brown

You've got to admire A.W. Brown's confidence in himself and his rights. He feels well and truly entitled to appeal to the whole towering edifice of government – not as a beggar, but by right, as a citizen of a democracy. There's an impressive faith in the goodwill of the ones on top to put things right.

I picture him at the kitchen table writing the letter on the small lined sheets of paper now in the file, his father looking on. He holds it up to the lamp to read the choicest parts: *Of course if you decide that this is a state of thing that should not be taken notice of . . .* he doesn't hold back on the ironic tone, and his father laughs.

Oh, and all that amateur legalese, that clumsy pompous nonsense trying to impress! *Five (5)*, as if the men at Bridge Street can't read. *Any street or thoroughfare* – has he really consulted the regulations about keeping pigs?

I'm laughing at silly, full-of-himself A.W. Brown because I've made up my mind about Joseph Connor. I've constructed a little story of an embattled man doing his best with some difficult circumstances. Still, I have to recognise that, under all his bluster, A.W. Brown is just stating what he can see: there are cattle and a pigsty on the school playground.

I have a densely packed folder on my computer called *Dear Sir letters*. Among many subjects dear to my heart, I've written about intrusive neighbourhood developments, climate change, the absence of girls on the back of the WeetBix boxes, and the heritage overlay that prevents me from installing solar panels.

Is it a distant muscle-memory of feudal *noblesse oblige* – the ones on the bottom trusting the ones on the top to look after them? Is it taking literally the idea of the *public servant*? We taxpayers are paying your salary, so listen when we speak. Or is it just the satisfaction of creating a few rotund phrases and getting the thing off your chest? Brown might have been a courageous whistleblower, the little man taking on the big one. But he might have just been a crackpot, like a person with a folder called *Dear Sir letters.*

Still, he's apparently found some allies among the people whose voices will count with the Department: parents at the school. Some of them are even willing to *be before you or your "Inspector" in support of this complaint.* That gives the Department no choice. Inspector Elliott is told to bring the parties together and make further enquiry.

Brown reiterates his complaint about the cattle on the playground and Connor reiterates his defence that the playground is *perfectly clean.* Connor brings up the *sectarian animosity* thing and Brown denies it. Two witnesses are called who are prepared to say that the *usual state* of the playground isn't objectionable.

It's a brief enquiry, and inconclusive. Then it's up to Inspector Elliott to make a judgement.

6th October 1890
Inspector Elliott to the Chief Inspector

Currabubula Public School: complaint against the teacher, final report.

The teacher is of opinion that this complaint is the result of religious animosity. He called no witness in support of this opinion, and the complainant gave it an unqualified denial.

The weak points in the complainant's case are that he fails to show that the teacher's use of the playground is injurious to the health of the pupils, that he has no children or relatives attending the school, and that he was unable to show that his complaint is a general one amongst the residents.

On the other hand, it must be said that the premises are kept scrupulously clean.

The complaint is in my opinion frivolous and brought forward by persons desirous of injuring the teacher. It appears to me desirable to extend to the teacher the sympathy and protection of the Minister.

I recommend that Mr Connor, Mr Brown and Mr Bradbury be informed as follows:

"After careful consideration, the Minister deems it unnecessary to interfere with the teacher's present arrangements as long as the premises are kept in their present clean and creditable condition."

A. Elliott

Inspector Elliott is going to great lengths to make this all sound very measured and even-handed. But is it really? All those animals and their poop in the playground: that's not really a *frivolous* complaint. Where's the proof that *persons* are *desirous of injuring the teacher*? If that's true, wouldn't it be relevant to ask why? And it's all very well to say that the playground was *scrupulously clean* on the day he saw it, but what about other days, when he wasn't expected? After all, even Connor admits that there were cows on the playground, and where there are cows, there's poop. But Elliott brushes past that. The Inspector can see nothing likely to interfere with the health and comfort of the pupils. But how hard was he looking?

I can see how his summary might strike a person as one-sided. In fact, what I think I'm hearing is ranks being closed.

27th November 1890

Petition from Currabubula residents to the Minister for Public Instruction

Sir,

We the undersigned have been informed that our esteemed teacher "Mr Connor" has been subjected to a series of annoyances as to the state of the school grounds by a person named Brown who has no connection whatever with our school. This man (Brown) we learn has written a number of letters to you – his tactics are quite apparent to us – he evidently intends to keep up an agitation so that though you may hold the teacher blameless you possibly might remove him for peace's sake.

Now Sir, we most emphatically protest against this man "Brown" interfering with the affairs of our school or teacher.

Mr Connor has been in charge of Currabubula School for the past six and a half years, and the efficient manner in which he has educated our children – the high character given him by the Inspector – together with his sobriety, honesty and industry are all so many facts that would cause us to exceedingly regret his removal – he having the entire respect of the parents and the just confidence of the children.

Mr Connor (whose family consists of ten) has by his saving and industry purchased some milking cows to keep his family in milk and butter. These cows are milked by his wife in his private yard which is kept thoroughly clean. We are of the opinion Sir that Mr Connor could not take a more effective method of setting a good example to his pupils, certainly more effective than by living in advance of his income.

If several teachers whom we have known had adopted Mr Connor's economic plan of bringing up large families thus some families would not be a burden on public charity after the death of the bread winner.

We earnestly entreat that our teacher <u>may not</u> be removed from us at the instigation of this rancorous intermeddler.

We are, Honorable Sir, Your obedient servants.

George Morris
Alfred Chidley
Jude McCarthy
James McCarthy
Michael McCarthy
Charles Horgan
A.C. Chidley
John Bourke
E. Horgan
F.G. Chidley
Herbert Cotton
G. Meakins
John Boyd
G.J. Boyd
J. McEnnis
R.J. Huxley
William Nolan
William Clendinnen
John McLachlan
Frederick Claypole
J.P. Moorby
J. Byrne

I have a confused sense of not having my right glasses on. These *obedient servants* are very exercised about something that A.W. Brown has never even mentioned: the removal of Joseph Connor. It's as if they're responding to the earlier letters, the forgeries. Those *were* about getting Connor removed. Is that why they see *tactics* in what, on the face of it, seems a straightforward complaint?

In any case, the petition runs right past the issue at hand, on another track altogether. The whole business of the cattle and the pigs and their poop and their stink has been left behind, replaced by a highflown allegory about thrift and improvidence, with Joseph Connor as the hero.

At the end of all this – five months' worth of backwards and forwards, Connor and Brown and Elliott and Bradbury all pulling in different directions – I have a baffled, blinded, smothered feeling. I want to be able to see the playground for myself. Stand there and look at the cart shed and the cow bail. How much cow poop is there? Can I smell the pigsty? Is it muddy and horrible or *dry* and *clean*?

Above all, I want to know what I should think about Joseph Connor. I'm still on his side, but I'm not sure I like him much. Not sure that I trust him much, either. A.W. Brown is starting to seem a bit of a buffoon and Bradbury is barely coherent, but they might be in the right.

Terrible Vale

Terrible Vale is a fold in the land that takes its name from the mountain above it called Terrible Billy. It's an hour or so on horseback south of Currabubula and the same distance north of the town of Werris Creek. Far from being terrible, the place is lovely. There's a sense of light, of a big sky opening overhead, of enormous quiet radiant space. To the west there's a long soft stretch of country where cattle graze under scattered trees, and in the far distance a line of dreamy blue mountains. Unlike at closed-in Currabubula, at Terrible Vale the eye can travel without obstacle into great distance.

Terrible Vale has never been an actual village. For a while it was a siding on the northern train line, with a few farmhouses off in the distance. Now there isn't even a siding. But in 1891 there were just enough children in the area for an application to be made for a school. As soon as the application was approved, some of the parents sent a letter to Inspector Elliott.

6th June 1891

Sir,
We, the parents of children about to attend the proposed new school at this place, humbly request that Miss B. Connor, pupil-teacher at the Public School Currabubula, be appointed as the teacher of our new school when erected. We have ascertained that Miss Connor would willingly accept the appointment if offered to her, and, that such appointment would be advantageous to the welfare of the school, we will endeavour to show by the following,–

1st all our children know Miss Connor, and many of them have been taught by her at Currabubula.

2nd there is no suitable place here at which a teacher could lodge: and, as the residence of Miss Connor's parents is only four miles from Terrible Vale, she would be able to ride to and fro morning and evening.

signed,
Charles Whyman
George Huxley
George Wright

Miss B. Connor, of course, was Bridie Connor. All the Terrible Vale children knew her because they were currently going to school at Currabubula, and for the last three years she'd been pupil-teacher there. She'd sped through the exams and was now ready to take on a school of her own. All those dreary hours of study would pay off at last. No more heartsink at the prospect of yet another page of sums, another page of parsing and analysis.

She'll have no competition for the job. The thing about being known to the children won't cut any ice with Inspector Elliott, but the thing about lodging will. Since there's *no suitable place* for a teacher to lodge near Terrible Vale, anyone sent to teach there would have to find lodgings at one of the nearest villages: Currabubula to the north or Werris Creek to the south. That would cost them. Even a male teacher, who could stay at the hotel in Currabubula or Werris Creek, could find he's got no money left at the end of the month, and would soon be requesting a transfer, or even deciding to leave the Service. Whereas Miss B. Connor can live at home for free. And as a woman, with no other employment prospects, she's likely to stay in the position until she marries. This is going to work out well for Inspector Elliott. His job is an endless game of musical chairs of too many schools and not enough teachers.

The only problem is that Bridie is too young. Departmental protocol is that a teacher should be at least seventeen, but she'll be sixteen for another four months – and the school needs a teacher straight away.

The Inspector has known her for a year. A mousey little thing, he's always thought, looks you in the eye and answers you smartly, but in a way that tells you she's been trained to it, not that it comes naturally. He's heard her father rapping out, Speak up, Bridie! Speak up, child!

It's true that she's young, but she's had plenty of experience of dealing with children, both as a pupil-teacher and at home. And of course, her father will be close by to keep an eye on things. It's a matter of an interview, he thinks. A chance to look at her properly and see if she'll be able to manage on her own out at Terrible Vale.

I'm imagining Bridie with the day so long trained for finally upon her. Is she nervous? Excited? Does she want to be a lady teacher, or would she rather be trying to set her cap at the right young man, the way all the other girls in the village are doing?

I'm sending her out of the house, over the railway line and up the hill into the bush to think about what's coming. She'll be away from home for the whole long day! In charge, with no one watching her and telling her how to do things! And money, actual money in her grown-up name, Bridget Connor, paid into the bank account that she'd open as soon as she turned seventeen! She feels herself expanding, her life taking on brilliant light and colour and swelling into the full size that her existence until now – as her father's obedient apprentice and her mother's dependable right hand – had never allowed.

This business of her age is a new kind of problem to solve. She doesn't have to show Inspector Elliott how much she knows about gerunds or the Norman Conquest. Seeming to be older than you are is both easier and harder.

The day the Inspector comes, Bridie's had her hair flattened and rolled and pinned away into a bun. It turns out that before she married, her mother was famous in Gulgong for helping women with their hair. She knows how to make the best of a plain face. Knows how to make your hair catch a man's eye. And how to make your hair say, I may only be sixteen but I am mature beyond my years.

They have some fun with it in the dark little bedroom, her mother for once lively, and not coughing as much as usual. When she comes towards Bridie holding a pair of Joseph's dress socks, she's laughing so hard there are tears in the corners of her eyes. She stuffs the socks down into Bridie's bodice and wiggles them about till they look convincing. No harm in making good better, she says. Nothing like a saucy bust to put years on a lass. She stands back, head tilted, amused at her little trick, and Bridie glimpses the playful girl she must once have been before too many children crowded out frivolity.

And drop your hanky, pet, when you hear him at the door, her mother says. Put a bit of colour in your cheeks. And pet, no smiling.

No need to warn her of that. This is no smiling matter. It's her life beginning.

16th July 1891
Inspector Elliott to the Chief Inspector

I have nominated Miss Connor for appointment to Terrible Vale for the following reasons:

1. Although she is barely 17 years of age she appears much older.
2. If she be appointed she will be able to reside with her parents.
3. A stranger will have considerable difficulty in obtaining suitable accommodation.
4. The parents of the probable pupils have sent an application for her appointment.

Under these special circumstances, I beg therefore to recommend the appointment of Miss Connor.

Archibald Elliott

I'm trying to remember what I was like when I was "barely 17". Would I have been robust enough to ride off every day to be in sole charge of a school, responsible for the education and wellbeing of twenty children? No, I was mooning about in a blur of adolescence, awkwardly trying to work out how to talk to boys and wondering if ironing my hair would make it straight.

Bridie Connor was made of sterner stuff. Smart and determined enough to ace those exams. Fearless enough to take on those kids and their parents, and the Department, with all the disadvantages of being female in a man's world.

I can imagine her enjoying the sense of openness and freedom that her new life at Terrible Vale promised. For the first time in her life, her days weren't spent *with none but the members of her own family*. For five days a week she was now away from all those brothers and sisters crammed into a house that was too small. Away from her weary mother and the obligation to help her. And perhaps especially, away from her father, that man who'd been with her night and day – as father, as teacher, as master – every single day of her life.

I've found a photo of Bridie at Terrible Vale Provisional School a few years after she began teaching there, standing beside the school-house with her pupils. She looks not only calm and authoritative, but happy, and so does the little group of children. She's standing very correctly, very straight, her hands behind her back. There's an impression of a strong clever face. Her dress crosses over a generous bosom, a real one now – or perhaps she always had one, the socks were my imagining, of course – and narrows to a tiny wasp waist. As Inspector Elliott says, she looks more mature than her years, and she looks like someone a child wouldn't take liberties with. I imagine her with a misbehaving pupil, listening in a watchful, steady way so the miscreant knows that excuses won't work. Cool, considering, judging, calm, unreadable. She watches the camera in the same way.

Now that Bridie has a school of her own, Currabubula needs a new pupil-teacher, but there's no need to look far. Bridie's brother Alfred is old enough to sit for the first pupil-teacher exams, and he seamlessly takes over from his sister.

23rd October 1891

Teacher's Report on Mr Alfred Connor, pupil-teacher on probation

Health: He is in good health. He has no physical infirmity that I am aware of. He has asked for no leave of absence since his appointment on probation.

Conduct out of school: His conduct out of school is blameless; his moral character is correct; he associates with no one outside the members of his own family. His leisure time is spent in taking healthy exercise, and in reading books of literary merit, for which he appears to have a great taste.

Conduct in school: Punctuality: Good
Diligence: Good
Obedience: Very good
Attention to duty: He is very painstaking with his class, and pays strict attention to his work.

Diligence in home study: His home lessons are well prepared, and he evinces much eagerness to give satisfaction.

Progress since last examination: He is making satisfactory advancement in the various sections of his studies since his appointment on probation.

Efficiency and usefulness: He pays strict attention to my instructions when examining his class, and spares no pains to effect such improvements as I point out. He is very useful in this school.

Has he received full instruction? He has received full instruction in all the prescribed subjects during the full specified time.

signed, J. Connor

Connor had been warm enough in his praise of Bridie, but Alfred gets a positively fulsome tone and more detail – all that about *reading books of literary merit.* For Alfred, being pupil-teacher wasn't a dead end, a kind of hobby till he got married. It was the start of a lifetime's serious career, with a reasonable salary and a professional ladder to climb. Behind him are the other children: Ernest at twelve is already being groomed to take over from Alfred when the time comes, and behind Ernest are Roland, Abigail, Adolphus, Louis and Beatrice, not to mention others still unborn. Joseph Connor has spawned a whole dynasty of schoolteachers. Teaching will give his children a future livelihood. Training them also gives him a constant supply of pupil-teachers over whose lives he has complete control.

Bridie had only been at Terrible Vale for three months when she writes to Inspector Elliott. It's the first time I hear her voice.

8th October 1891
Bridget Connor to Inspector Elliott

Sir, there being no enclosure at this school wherein to keep a horse, I am obliged to travel by train to and fro daily between Currabubula and Terrible Vale, a distance of four miles.

There is no place in the vicinity of my school at which I may lodge, hence I am compelled to live with my parents at Currabubula.

The payment of railway fares is a considerable drain upon my salary. I have therefore the honour, Sir, to apply for a free pass by rail between Currabubula and Terrible Vale for the purpose of attending my school.

I have the honour to be, Sir, your humble servant
B. Connor
Teacher

At first glance this letter looked like such a mild, dull little thing, her request so unimportant, that I nearly didn't bother to transcribe it. Needing a place to put the horse doesn't sound unreasonable. On the other hand, couldn't you just tie it up, or hobble it? But Bridie Connor knows more about horses than I do. If she says she needs an enclosure, then I suppose she must.

But now I'm looking again, there's something odd hidden under this letter's bland surface. It's that vehement word, *compelled. I am compelled to live with my parents*. Maybe it doesn't mean anything. She'd already used *obliged* and would have been taught not to repeat words. *Compelled* could just be what was called Elegant Variation. Or is it someone writing her first letter to an official, and in her inexperience getting the tone a bit wrong?

Still ... *compelled.* The word jumps out from her letter with the force of suppressed violence. It's one of those words that comes out of your mouth without your planning it. It might be telling you a truth you hadn't brought to consciousness.

12th October 1891
Inspector Elliott to the Chief Inspector

I know no reason why Miss Connor should be granted a free railway pass. She was recommended for her present appointment on the understanding that she would be able to live at home.

I recommend that Miss Connor be informed that it is not the practice of the Department to grant free railway passes to teachers, and that when teachers do not live near their school they are expected to make suitable arrangements for the proper performance of their duties.

A. Elliott

Margin:
Mr Inspector Elliott

Is the teacher's statement that no lodgings are available near her school correct?

J.M.G., Chief Inspector, 15-10-91

It's true that Miss Connor got the job on the understanding that she could live at home and ride to work. But no one had thought about the lack of a horse enclosure. The original understanding had a mistake in it, a forgotten factor, and Miss Connor was suggesting a way of fixing it.

School pupils could apply for a train pass if they lived too far from the nearest school. It doesn't seem a big stretch to let a teacher have one too, when she was *compelled* to live an hour's ride away.

21st October 1891

Inspector Elliott to the Chief Inspector

Her statement is correct. The only suitable family with whom she could board lives one and a half miles from the school, and that family objects to boarders.

When Miss Connor was nominated for the position this matter was discussed.

A. Elliott

Chief Inspector: I recommend that this application be declined. 26-10-91

This matter was discussed. Yes, but now the Chief Inspector is wondering about it. The petitioners originally said there was *no suitable place here at which a teacher could lodge*, which sounded unremarkable. Perhaps they didn't have any space in their modest little farmhouses. Or it might have been awkward to have the teacher living with some of her pupils in the enforced intimacy of a small house, although even as late as the 1960s, teachers in remote places often had to bunk in with a local household. It could be that the local wives didn't want her under the same roof as their sons and husbands. Bridie might have been prettier than she looks in the photos.

In the end the Chief Inspector has no choice but to decline the application. If Bridie Connor got a train pass, every teacher would soon be asking for one.

So . . . what might have happened, had the Department given Bridie a rail pass? It occurs to me that, as well as being saved an 8-mile ride every day, she'd also have had an alternative to living at home. The town of Werris Creek is the same distance south of Terrible Vale as Currabubula is to the north. But it's a bigger place. In Werris Creek she'd have been able to find somewhere respectable enough for a young woman to board, and with a free train pass, she'd have been able to afford it. If for any reason Bridget Connor wanted not to be *compelled* to live at home, a pass would have made it possible.

And now I'm thinking about the horse. Some of the pupils at Terrible Vale must have had to ride to school. Why not ask the Department for a horse enclosure, for the pupils as well as the teacher, rather than a rail pass?

I'm wondering whether Bridie didn't want the problem of the horse enclosure solved. She wanted a rail pass. And might she be doing that so she wasn't *compelled* to live at home?

9th December 1891
The Evening News, Sydney

Currabubula. This village, on the railway line, is but seldom mentioned in the Town & Country Journal, but its people wake up now and again and do something.

Recently, Miss Connor, teacher of the Terrible Vale school, gave her pupils a picnic. Mr John Boyd, the wealthy farmer, lent one of his paddocks, and cleared a large shed for the convenience of the merrymakers. All the usual diversions of a country feast day were indulged in, not omitting even dancing on the green to the entrancing strains of a bush accordion. The various repasts were excellent in quality and abundant in quantity, good humour prevailed: and all the folk engaged passed a most enjoyable day. The crops about Currabubula look splendid, and an excellent harvest should reward the efforts of the hard-working farmer. So far there is no sign of rust in the wheat, and the hayfields are very fine. Mr George Lindley, the local blacksmith, and Mrs Michael McCarthy, both esteemed residents, have

```
departed this life. At Piallaway Station shearing is
being done with machine, where the yield this year is
unusually heavy and of fine quality.
```

Isn't there a picnic in a Jane Austen book where a wealthy farmer, as part of his courtship of the main character, entertains a party of people? They pick strawberries and get hot? If this were a Jane Austen novel – actually if it were any novel at all – even the dullest reader would pick up the author's signal: *John Boyd is about to become a love interest.*

But in 1891 John Boyd was forty-two and married for a second time (his first wife had died in childbirth). He had eight children, three of whom were Miss Connor's pupils. He seems to have been on every committee in the place – for the Grand Templars, for the Union Church, for the application for a railway siding at Terrible Vale. In a novel, none of that would put him out of the running for being a love interest, but somehow I don't want to wrestle him into that role. I think he was just one of those energetic, public-spirited people who get good things done in their community. (That does make me wonder about the horse enclosure, though. He'd have got one up like a shot if he'd known it was a problem.)

So, if Bridie Connor's heart beat faster at the sight of some beloved, it mightn't have been John Boyd. And what with running a school single-handedly and being *compelled* to go on living at home, she mightn't have had much opportunity to think about romance.

Which is a shame. I'd thought sentimentally about a nice little story about the reserved young schoolteacher and the warm-hearted farmer. Made for TV! But it's not what happened.

Blistered Hands and Back-Ache

In 1890 the Department of Public Instruction decided to encourage the planting of trees on school grounds by establishing a yearly Arbor Day. The idea was that a school community would chip in for saplings provided by the Department, and do the work of planting them. It was partly practical – the children needed shade. But it might also have been designed to encourage a stronger sense of ownership among the people in the village for their public school. The schoolhouse was a visible symbol of the power and reach of a government that was increasingly intruding into people's lives. Establishing Arbor Day and providing saplings to every school was a way of demonstrating the benign aspect of that intrusion.

When I first visited Currabubula, in 2009, the perimeter of the playground was picked out with half-a-dozen pepper trees. They were old and venerable, huge trees with trunks bumpy and dimpled with age, a whole long convoluted history right there in the bark. They were graceful trees and cast a deep shade that generations of children at the school must have been glad of.

20th August 1891
Joseph Connor to the Under-Secretary

Sir,
I have the honour to inform you that I have planted all my trees except one, which I am reserving for tomorrow.

This will make 46 trees, all looking well and securely guarded with strong wire netting. I have also made a nursery in which I have planted about 80 trees and should any of the others fail I will be able to transplant from my nursery next year the kinds of trees which my own observation in the meantime will enable me to select as most suitable to the locality.

J. Connor

These would surely be the trees that I saw a hundred and something years later. What innocent enthusiasm Joseph Connor is full of here. The Under-Secretary isn't likely to be interested in the *strong wire netting*, let alone the whole business of the *little nursery*, but Connor can't stop himself boasting, in a small way, about what he's doing.

27th August 1891
Joseph Connor to Inspector Elliott

Accounts for tree-planting at this school.

The total increments amounted to eight pounds, all received by me by subscriptions.

The total disbursements amount to sixteen pounds, for which please find bills attached, except for 5/2 for which I am myself accountable, and which sum I have paid, as well as the balance of difference between disbursements and increments.

Following is statement of expenditure:

M. McCarthy, labour	4-1/9
W. Sullivan, labour	2-10/-
A.J. Barton, timber	2-10/-
J. Byrne, nails etc.	11/-
D. Hughes, wire netting	7/-
Carriage on netting	14/9-
Lassetter, netting & carriage	4-19/6-
Telegram	1/-
Two post office orders	1/2-
Note paper	6d
Stamps	2/6
Total:	16 pounds

I trenched the whole of the ground myself, knowing that the funds at my disposal would be far from sufficient to do the amount of work I would have liked to carry out; I have been engaged in this work for the past three months, and spent the whole of my mid-winter holidays at it, and, though I suffered frequently with blistered hands and back-ache, it was withal a labour of love.

I have planted out 46 trees, all securely guarded with a strong frame-work of wood, surrounded by two and a half inch mesh, 16 gauge, galvanised, five feet wide, wire netting. All those trees were planted and doing well before Arbor Day excepting one which was reserved for the occasion.

I have also made a nursery in which I have some 80 trees looking splendidly, and securely fenced in for future use.

I have supervised the whole of the work not done by myself, and insisted on its being faithfully performed.

I have now the honour, sir, to apply for a refund of 8 pounds, which sum I have paid in excess of the amount received by subscription.

I have etc.

J. Connor

For the first time, I can hear a personal tone, and as a bit of a tree planter myself, I'm warming to Joseph Connor again. Here's a man who doesn't mind getting his hands dirty. In fact, it sounds as though he relishes the work. What a relief, how simple and satisfying, to dig a hole rather than trying to explain the lowest common denominator to kids who couldn't care less. Perhaps it was in his Irish childhood that he learned how to dig, how to plant, how to stand back at the end of the day, aching and covered with good honest dirt, with a sense of a job well done. He's forty-six years old – he knows he won't be around when the trees reach maturity. It's not even his own place. As a teacher he knows he could be moved any time it suited the Department.

Good on you, Joseph Connor, for going to so much trouble to raise money among the parents to plant those pepper trees, keeping one so there could be something of a ceremony on Arbor Day. See? I want to tell that *evil and malicious* person. He was a good man, putting his heart and soul into selflessly making the playground a better place for the next hundred years.

23rd November 1891
Joseph Connor to Inspector Elliott

Sir,
I have the honour to apply for twenty small buckets and a watering-pot to water the trees at the school. The water has to be carried a considerable distance from the creek, and, if I had those buckets, I could, by the aid of the biggest male pupils, water the trees in an hour after school closing. I have tried borrowing buckets, but this plan keeps the boys too late from their homes.

The watering-pot is necessary as, throwing water on from a bucket, displaces the soil from near the roots of the young trees.

Appended please find an estimate which would total 1-13/6, and I dare say the carriage or railway freight would amount to about 2/-, making the whole cost 1-15/6.

I have etc.
J. Connor

25th November 1891
Inspector Elliott to Joseph Connor

Mr Connor:

Would it not be preferable to have water drawn from the creek by a horse, and would not the people assist in the matter without aid from the Department?

A. Elliott

28th November 1891
Joseph Connor to Inspector Elliott

Sir, Drawing water would be preferable to carrying it, but such a course would be impracticable, as the horse would have to be run in after the dismissal of the school, leaving no time afterwards for watering.

The residents evince no desire to assist in watering those trees, and I would much sooner do it myself than run the almost certain risk of a refusal.

The apparatus I have applied for, if granted, would leave me dependent on no one, would be a safeguard against the certain destruction of the young trees during the summer heat, and would be taken good care of as the property of the Minister.

J. Connor

The residents evince no desire to assist in watering those trees. Wait, aren't these the same people who raised the not-trivial sum of eight pounds, just a few months earlier, towards the cost of planting and fencing them? Having done that were they happy to watch the little trees die?

Let's imagine it: Joseph Connor setting off towards the blacksmith's. He's pretending he needs, oh, a buckle for a harness. He's hoping he'll run into someone who subscribed to the Arbor Day fund, and sure enough, there's a knot of men around the forge. A bit of chit-chat – he starts with the weather, of course, and that brings him quite naturally around to the coming summer, and the slips of trees newly planted that'll need watering through their first hot season.

They know what he wants. But no one says, oh yes, Joe, I'll give you a hand. There's that vibrating little silence that happens when everyone knows what everyone else is thinking but no one's going to say it.

From his years in the classroom Connor knows that you only get an answer from a group if you single out one of the blank faces watching you. Now, Jack, he says to Teddy Thwaites's father. Jack Thwaites had given five shillings to the subscription. What about it, Jack, think you might give me a hand with the watering?

Jack looks away, clears his throat, scuffs his foot in the dry dust of the blacksmith's floor. Ar well, he says. It sounds as if there's going to be more, but there isn't. Herb Cotton steps away from the little circle to spit into the grass outside, Bob Goodsir flaps at a fly and uses the movement to move towards the doorway, Jim Bollard stares at the empty road as if there's something interesting there.

Joseph Connor's holding his hat, he'd taken it off when he'd stepped into the shade of the smithy, and now the phrase *cap in hand* comes to him, and the image of himself standing there begging. Feels his mouth tighten and a hot cloud of rage and humiliation warms him. Claps the hat back on his head, stalks out. Feels them watching him all the way back up the road to the school. He tries to walk naturally, normally, but thinks he can hear a muttered comment and a snigger, and somehow he's forgotten how to walk, knows that if he turns around he'll see them lined up outside the smithy, watching the strange way his bottom's moving in his pants.

The apparatus I have applied for, if granted, would leave me dependent on no one.

He loves those little trees. But he won't beg. Won't open himself again to be humiliated. Even if someone comes forward to offer now, he won't be beholden. Not to any of them. Won't be dependent on their goodwill. Which isn't there.

And that's peculiar, isn't it? Between the gathering of a generous subscription from the residents, and the need for some help two months later, some dark thing has fallen. Something about the trees, or Joseph Connor planting them, or Joseph Connor asking for help, has gone in a weird direction.

I can imagine the scene at the blacksmith's. What I can't imagine is what everyone's thinking. Why would no one help water the trees that the village has come together to buy and plant? What went wrong in Currabubula in November 1891?

30th November 1891
Inspector Elliott to the Chief Inspector

There are about 70 trees at the Currabubula School growing well. The teacher takes great pride in them and deserves encouragement.

I recommend that he be allowed the sum of 1-15/6 for the purchase of buckets and a watering can.

A. Elliott

Inspector Elliott made sure Connor got the buckets, and that's why, over a hundred years later, I could admire the pepper trees in the playground. Sadly, when I went back a few years later, they'd been cut down. According to a local, they were *full of rot and a hazard*. The stumps were ground down so thoroughly that no trace of them can be found now. Only the photos I took on that first trip show that they were ever there.

Have Not Got It

Public education was theoretically free, but the men who'd framed the Act thought that parents mightn't value education if it cost them nothing, so they ruled that a token amount – threepence a week per child – should be paid. The teacher had to collect the fees, actual coins into his actual hand. It must have been awkward. The handing-over of grubby coins made the teacher not so much a gift to the community as a kind of shopkeeper.

Worse than awkward, really, because as well as being shopkeeper, the teacher was also the debt collector. If the parents didn't pay, the teacher had to chase them.

A parent could apply for an exemption if he or she couldn't afford the threepence a week. But the greatest awkwardness in this arrangement was that it was the teacher who decided whether or not you qualified for the exemption.

26th February 1892
<u>Return of School Fees in Arrears for the month ending 26th February 1892</u>

This return should be prepared, and transmitted to the local Inspector on the last Friday in each month. In every case in which arrears are continuously increasing, the teacher should furnish a report to the local Inspector on the special report form provided for the purpose. A teacher who steadily insists on weekly payments, ought to give the Department little or no trouble in regard to debts for school fees.

Teacher's Report upon the character and circumstances of the applicant

Name and address of debtor: Christopher Kelly, Currabubula
Occupation: Labourer
Amount and source of income: 80 pounds, by labour
Debtor's present circumstances: Cannot say, nearly always employed
Amount of debt: Eight shillings
Dates between which debt has accrued: 13-1-92 to 8-3-92
What efforts have been made to collect it? 1st a bill, 2nd personal interview
Have you tried to obtain payment by instalments? Yes
Number of children to be supported: Six
Alleged cause of inability to pay fees: "Have not got it."
Your opinion of such cause: Believe he could pay the school fees.

Mr Christopher Kelly, the applicant in this instance, is a respectable man. He lives by his labour, but he has been in constant work, and the recipient of regular wages during the past six months, and should, I think, be able to afford paying the school fees. Mr Kelly has been exempt from the payment of fees during the past two years. He evidently supposes that he should be always exempt.

Having inquired into the circumstances of this case, I consider that the applicant is able to pay School fees, and that, therefore, his request should be not allowed.

J. Connor

I'm looking aslant at Joseph Connor's judgement here. Kelly was a labourer. His work would generally have been irregular, the payment modest. He was supporting eight people on what he earned. For two years Connor had given him an exemption from fees. Was Kelly suddenly earning more in 1892 than he had in 1890 or 1891?

I think it's more likely that something's happened in the last year, or some longstanding irritation has reached a tipping point. Connor's lost his sympathy for Kelly and he's decided to wield the power he has. *He evidently supposes that he should be always exempt.* There's a mocking, sarcastic tone to that. Connor is angry.

12th March 1892
From Inspector Elliott to the Chief Inspector

It appears from the Teacher's Report that Mr Kelly is well able to pay school fees.

I recommend that his application be declined and that he be informed that unless he pays all fees due on or before the 31st inst, legal proceedings will be taken to recover the same.

A. Elliott

What would it be like to have four children in your class whose father had just been threatened with legal action because of you? Wouldn't it be a bit hard to look them in the eye and patiently explain again about the subjunctive?

It would be your own doing. You'd lost your temper, filled out the form in a rosy glow of indignation, put the stamp on the envelope and sent it off while the words were still hot. Now you had to spend every day under the hard eyes of the Kelly children, and feel the turning away of people in the village. Believing that you were in the right wouldn't be much consolation.

A wise man would have found a way to back away. *On further enquiry* … There'd be some excuse to withdraw the report, patch things up. But Joseph Connor doesn't seem to be that man.

I'm back to where I started all that time ago in the Archives. I opened the file and read those nasty letters and wanted to know what was going on. I was inclined to favour Joseph Connor then, thought of him as a straightforward, honest fellow doing his guileless best. Now a dozen little things have left a residue, like a grubby bathring, round my picture of him. There were the poison-pen letters, and the revolving door of pupil-teachers. There were the difficulties in getting anyone to fix the water tank or clean out the dunnies. There was the complaint about the playground, and Connor's slipperiness in defending himself. There's Bridie using that vehement word *compelled* and the odd way no one is willing to help him water the Arbor Day saplings.

Maybe there's nothing here at all. Maybe I'm over-listening. Looking too hard for drama in all these not-terribly-dramatic letters, when it's nothing more than human beings rubbing up against each other in perfectly ordinary ways.

Still, I can't let go of the feeling that something's happening in Currabubula, and Joseph Connor's at the centre of it.

PART TWO

Bruised and Blackened

16th June 1892

John Bradbury to the Minister for Public Education

Sir I should like to call your attention to the treatment the children of Currabubula State School get from the Master Mr Connor.

they have their hands Bruised and Blackened with the Cane and Sometimes Caught by the neck and flogged on the Back and legs and Black marks left.

One girl over 13 years had been caned 4 times one day and Black marks left on her hands and caned the day following on her sore hands and my Girl nearly 14 years was often treated similar till I took her away also my little girl about 6 year in 4 day following recived 22 lashes my eldest Boy had the first finger of his right hand Blackened and he has had Whitlow and lost the first Joint thiss is but a show of his Crueltys the same Crueltys have been carried on for years these and many others of similar charges I can Prove

I cannot think that Masters are alowed to treat children as their temper leads them if so I will withdraw my children and I think in the Face of Civilization my son should have Compensation for the loss of his Finger

Honorable Sir I beg that you will do your best to hinder such Crueltys

I am at your service in this matter
Respectfully yours
John Bradbury

I had to look up what a whitlow is – it's an infection of the fingertip, usually starting around the nail. These days it can be cured, but in 1892 there was no good treatment. It's plausible that an infection could have been triggered by a caning, as Bradbury is suggesting, and that an infected fingertip could result in the loss of part of the finger.

Hitting the finger rather than the palm could be an accident, but the general picture Bradbury is drawing sounds terrible, even by the spare-the-rod-and-spoil-the-child standards of the day. But is it true? His letter is the voice of a man spluttering with confused rage. And what about that wild flourish of *in the Face of Civilization*? On first reading I thought, Oh, this is just a rant. But when I take a moment to put in a few commas and fullstops, I see that John Bradbury is stating the facts as he's observed them. He's naming who and when, and how many, on what part of the body.

The Act had some details about corporal punishment:

Corporal punishment may be inflicted, but by the Principal Teacher only, or by an Assistant with his approval. It should be restricted as much as possible to extreme cases; and the Teacher must keep a record of the time and place of punishment, its amount, and the nature of the offence.

The frequent infliction of such punishment will be regarded as evidence of a Teacher's want of disciplinary power. The boxing of pupils' ears is strictly forbidden,

```
as is also the infliction of corporal punishment upon
female pupils 12 years of age and over.
```

The vague wording made it hard to know the exact boundaries of what was permissible, but it was better than what had happened before, when teachers had been free to do pretty much whatever they wanted. A few conventions fleshed out the bones of the Act. A light cane – a length of thin bamboo – was generally used to administer the "slaps", and it was commonly understood that they should be limited to the hands, that too many slaps shouldn't be given, and that they shouldn't be given too often. Punishment was allowed to be painful, but it wasn't allowed to cause real damage. Whatever was doled out was supposed to be recorded in the Punishment Book, a formal ledger supplied to teachers. All this seemed a way of keeping teachers in check, but of course only the teacher and the pupils in the classroom knew what actually happened.

I was never given any corporal punishment at school, but many of my contemporaries – others who grew up in the 1950s – tell gruesome stories of brutal childhood canings in the classroom, not restricted to *extreme cases*. Plenty of parents, even then, still saw physical punishment as a normal part of child-rearing. My childhood friend Annette took me into her parents' bedroom one day to show me the "strap" her father regularly used on her and her sister. It was a heavy leather belt hanging on a hook on the back of the door, a curling, frightening thing. For Annette and her sister it was part of the accepted way of things between a father and his children, but she knew there was no ugly dark thing on the back of my parents' door. She was looking forward to seeing me shocked.

Thomas Bradbury has suffered lasting physical damage, so his father's accusations are serious enough to warrant a formal, courtroom-like enquiry. The complainants and the defendant come together in the schoolroom, with Inspector Elliott presiding and taking down the evidence. Witnesses are called in to say their piece and be cross-examined. It's not a court of law, but it's set up to feel as impartial and just as one.

25th June 1892
Enquiry into charges made by Mr Bradbury against Joseph Connor, teacher at Currabubula Public School.

<u>Depositions of the Complainants, Bradbury, Huxley, Clarke and Webb</u>

Mr Bradbury said:

I am 40 years of age. I live about a mile from Currabubula and I am a farmer.

I have heard my children and others say that pupils are caught by the neck and flogged on the back and legs. Mr Charles Webb showed me his daughter's hands. On one hand there were two bruises on the fleshy part of the thumb; on the other there was a bruise at the first joint of the little finger. It was the 15th inst when I saw those marks.

My own children have come home on several occasions with their hands bruised. Two years ago last October my eldest girl Agnes came home with 3 marks as wide as a finger on her hand which she could not close for 3 days. Since then she has not been cane marked but she has come home day after day stating that she has been caned.

During the last school week of last year my youngest child Jane received 22 lashes, 6 on Tuesday, Wednesday and Thursday respectively, and 4 on Friday.

I can see this. This is no woolly blustering, it's dates and dimensions, something you can feel the heft of. Bradbury isn't a man of education, he doesn't write things down, but people who don't do much writing often have good memories, and I believe him here. Certainly you'd remember your little girl coming home four days in a row having been *lashed*. Still, I also can't really believe it. How could Connor – a grown man – hit a little seven-year-old girl six times? Then do it again the day after, and the day after that? With sixty or seventy other children looking on? The child crying, cringeing, cowering, calling out *Please, sir! Please, sir!*

> Since Easter my eldest boy Thomas came home one night and showed me his first finger on the right hand: there was a mark as black as coal near the first joint. I took no notice at the time, but shortly after the finger began to fester, a whitlow was formed, the bone to the first joint has come out.
>
> I complained to Mr Connor at the time regarding these matters, and accepted his apology, on the understanding that there would be no further cause of complaint.

So like any good parent, Mr Bradbury goes up to the school to complain. Fronts up to Connor and gets an apology. *I accept, Mr Bradbury, that I may have been a little harsh on the children.* Shaking hands, avoiding each other's eyes like dogs not sure of each other. There'd been that earlier business, after all – the cattle in the playground that Bradbury had claimed were diseased.

Connor's standing on the front step of the school, watching Bradbury clump in his big boots down the track worn in the grass to where his horse is tied up to the post, nosing the water in the trough. The drops glitter in its whiskers in the late-afternoon sun. He goes on watching as Bradbury gets on, turns the horse, its big brown rump moving up and down and the tail hanging down, a bit of thistle caught in the tip, till horse and man go down where the road slopes into the gully and across the creek, out of sight behind the willows.

Now Connor gets to cross-examine Bradbury.

> Examined by Mr Connor:
>
> About last Christmas twelve months I signed a petition which complained of your using the playground as a run for cattle. I can't remember how many signatures were on the paper – mine may have been the first. After I had signed the petition I wrote a letter to the Minister stating that I thought a change of master would be beneficial to the school. The Minister's reply was in substance that the case was settled and there would be no change at present.

I imagine that Connor has asked about the petition of complaint in order to establish that Bradbury has a history of hostility towards him. Bradbury was the first to sign, and then he went further – he wrote to the Minister. Inspector Elliott, listening and making notes, would understand what Connor was establishing: *Bradbury is trouble*.

Then comes this:

> I have punished my boy William with the thong of a bullock whip. I marked his legs but not his face.
>
> signed, John Bradbury

So this man – the man accusing Connor of slapping his pupils too much – took to another of his sons with a bullock whip! And thinks it's all right because he didn't mark his face! Outrageous, barbaric, unspeakable.

But how has this awful thing come into this enquiry? Well, it's here because Connor has put it here. Inspector Elliott doesn't record the questions that Connor asks, but they must have been something like, *Do you ever punish your boys? What do you punish them with? Have you ever left marks?* Connor has asked the questions knowing the answer, casting his cunning fly far out into the stream so he can bring this damning thing back and hold it up for all to see. It's like *Brown shot his brother dead.* It's from somewhere beyond the room and the facts, nothing whatsoever to do with Thomas and his infected finger.

Someone must have given this gem to Joseph Connor. *A word in your ear, Connor.* A quiet corner one sunny Saturday afternoon after the meeting of the Trustees of the Common. One man to another. *I see you're having a bit of trouble with Bradbury. Well, it might interest you to know ...*

Or did Connor dig it up all by himself? He gets Thomas to stay back at school one day and asks him, *Does your father ever punish you or your brother?* A shrug and a sticking-out of the bottom lip. *Sometimes.* Connor silky, inviting. *Oh? And what does he use, Thomas? His belt? What does he do it with, Thomas?*

Outrageous, barbaric, unspeakable. My response is exactly what Connor wants. He's planned it and he's brought it into being.

Mrs Huxley deposed: My name is Margaret Huxley. I am 35 years of age, and my husband is a farmer.

My boy, George, has been marked on the legs with a cane, and punished on the head. His ears have been dragged. I have seen marks on children's hands. I have seen marks on Martha Jane Webb and Dave Clarke and Abner Clarke. My own girl Gertrude Huxley has had her ears pulled.

These accusations are specific, they have the weight of the real. Mrs Huxley can specify the parts of the body, the implement that did the striking.

Examined by Mr Bradbury: You have not influenced me in the evidence I have given. I do not know that you are intimate with Mrs Clarke or Mrs Webb, and you are not intimate with me.

I suppose Bradbury is trying to establish the impartiality of Mrs Huxley's evidence, but it's an unfortunate form of words. I can imagine Connor smirking. Then it's his turn to give her a grilling, and he springs something new on her.

Examined by Mr Connor: I have not heard of my boys fighting on the way home.

He's got Mrs Huxley flustered enough for her to say she knows nothing about it, and that's surely her wriggling on Connor's baited hook, because what boys have never fought on the way home from school?

Examined by the Inspector: I have complained to Mr Connor about his treatment of my children. I have called on him once and my husband has seen him once or twice. When my eldest boy was punished I wrote to the

Police Magistrate at Tamworth, but I received no reply and no one came to me regarding my letter.

signed, Margaret Huxley

This is far more than the usual grizzling among parents. Mrs Huxley has fronted up to Connor and had it out with him face to face. That hasn't changed things, so her husband tries, perhaps twice. Then she takes the quite extreme step of complaining, in writing, to the police magistrate. Mrs Huxley would have known, as any parent does, that complaining about a teacher is risky. A teacher can make life hell for a child in ways that leave no marks. But the situation is bad enough for Mr Bradbury, and now Mrs Huxley, Mrs Webb and Mrs Clarke, to stick their necks out and be part of this public hearing.

Mrs Clarke deposed: My name is Sarah Clarke. I am 44 years of age. My husband is employed on Piallaway Station. I am not related to either Mr Connor or Mr Bradbury.

My boy Abner has been slapped about the head and marked on the neck. His ears have been pulled. My boy Dave has been similarly treated, and my eldest girl disliked school so much owing to Mr Connor's treatment that I had great trouble to get her to attend.

Examined by Mr Connor: I am not aware of my boys fighting on the way home. I have heard that Dave cut your wire fence. I got the fence repaired to save trouble.

signed, Sarah Clarke

Connor tries the fighting-on-the-way-home thing again, before pouncing on her with something more serious: the business of cutting the fence. Mrs Clarke doesn't try to bluster or deny. She admits it: *I have heard that Dave cut your wire fence.* Then without fuss she lays down an ace that swings the game back her way: *I got the fence repaired to save trouble.*

I once heard a barrister talking about the tricks of cross-examination. If it's a bloke, he said, I start off by asking them to tell me their children's birthdays. They can never tell me. It gets them off balance, and that's where I want them. The red herrings that Connor tosses in have nothing to do with the case at hand, but they unbalance his accusers and taint their sons. If they fight on the way home and cut people's fences, they might also be lying about how the teacher treats them.

> Mrs Webb deposed: My name is Alice Webb. I am 32 years of age. My husband is a boundary rider on Piallaway.
>
> My eldest girl Lilian Jane has been severely punished by Mr Connor. She was caned on the hand last Monday week. She told me that she received 3 beatings – 2 slaps each time. She was caned 4 times on Tuesday and 4 times on Wednesday. She has marks on her hands now.

This is all so specific I have to believe it. But of course, these mothers know each other well – they all live on Piallaway Station and their husbands work there. It's easy to imagine them getting together and making sure their stories are consistent.

> Examined by the Inspector: After my child had been caned the third time my husband called on Mr Connor, who said he was sorry for caning the girl. The child was however punished twice the next day.
>
> signed, Alice Webb

Would a teacher really face up to an angry parent, apologise, and yet not be able to stop himself doing the same thing the very next day?

Mr Gould deposed: My name is Alfred Gould. I am 52 years of age and I am a farm labourer by occupation. I have two children attending the school. Mr Connor has never punished either of them.

Examined by Mr Bradbury: About 5 years ago I saw two marks on the wrist of Vincent Boots. I saw a mark on the ear of Gertrude Huxley about a fortnight ago. I had an enquiry held at the school some 5 years ago into Mr Connor's charge against one of my step-children, Anne Cheetham, who was accused of bad writing in the WC. I was not satisfied with the result of the enquiry and sent my girl afterwards to Werris Creek School to finish her schooling.

signed, Alfred Gould

The enquiry about *bad writing in the WC* – I assume obscenities – isn't in the file. But it means that this is at least the third enquiry into Joseph Connor – the one about the playground, the one about the *bad writing*, and now this one. It sounds as if Connor was cleared of the complaint Gould brought, but Gould felt strongly enough against Joseph Connor to move his stepdaughter to a school much further away, which must have created all sorts of inconveniences.

Evidence of witnesses for the complainants

Thomas Bradbury deposed: I am 12 years of age, and Mr Bradbury the complainant is my father.

I have been caned by Mr Connor but not very often. Mr Connor left a mark on my finger about 7 weeks ago.

There was no sore on my finger when Mr Connor caned me. Soon after getting caned I felt my finger sore when I had to write. I have had my finger tied up about 5 weeks.

Examined by Mr Connor: I told Charlie Milburne and some other boys in the playground after the caning that my finger was sore. I showed them the finger.

Examined by the Inspector: I do not remember hurting my finger in any other way.

signed, Thomas Bradbury

This is odd, isn't it? Thomas's father is accusing Connor of excessive punishment, but Thomas says he doesn't get caned very often.

Jane Bradbury deposed: I am 7 years old, and Mr Bradbury, the complainant, is my father. I am a pupil at Currabubula School.

When I am naughty in the classroom Mr Connor canes me. He never gives me more than 2 slaps, sometimes only 1. I do not get the cane more than once in the day. I do not remember him ever marking my hands.

signed, Jane Bradbury

This is even odder. Jane's father has said she received twenty-two lashes over four days, but she says she never gets more than two in a day.

It could be that their father is making up the numbers, fabricating the case against Connor. But it's possible the children are more frightened of Connor than they are of their father, and it's them doing the fabricating. Thomas has two more years of sitting in that classroom, six hours a day, five days a week. Jane has seven years to go. No wonder they're cautious.

Abner Clarke deposed: I am 12 years old, and I am no relative of either Mr Connor or Mr Bradbury. I attend Currabubula School.

Mr Connor has punished me on the head, hands and back. The last time he punished me was on the back. He has marked my face with the cane and with the ring he has on his hand.

Examined by Mr Connor: I have never had a fight on my way home from school.

signed, Abner Clarke

I absolutely believe the detail about the ring. It's something about the form of words: not just *his ring*, but *the ring he has on his hand.* Joseph Connor's hand is suddenly real to me. I can see the thick fingers, the scattering of dark hairs between the knuckles, the big flat fingernails none too clean. But how does a ring mark a person's face? A wedding ring is surely too flush with the skin. A signet ring would leave a mark, but only if the person wearing it slapped backhand.

What would it be like, to slap someone across the face backhand? There'd be a feeling of power, but power only just controlled, because with backhand, beyond a certain degree of torque, momentum takes over. There'd be a feeling of surrender. Wild, exuberant, reckless, exhilarating.

As someone whose profession is making things up, I don't think that a boy would make up a detail like the ring. In a way, the difficulty of imagining how a ring would leave a mark is proof of its truth.

As a child I was hit only once, but I still remember it. Dad's sitting in the big armchair listening to an LP, a woman warbling through some classical thing. I'm pestering him for ... what? What I really want is his attention, though I'm probably asking for something simpler. The record has a photo of the singer on the cover, Irmgard Seefried. The eye of memory sees her: a fleshy beauty with a dark pixie haircut, showing a lot of plush German bosom. Somehow, at six or seven, I know how to get Dad's attention. I pick up the record cover and flap it at him and crow, "Who's the pretty lady?" He gets up out of the chair and slaps me across the behind – quite hard, though not painfully, and only the once. But the shock, the affront of it, and the power of it! His power, to do that physical thing to me – but my power, too, to cut through his reserve, make him lose control! It's like the sun running backwards.

So I have the flicker of an impulse to defend Connor here. A defiant twelve-year-old, already nearly as tall as he was, and everyone watching. The boy could have the last word, or Connor could. A long hot day of being patient. Then the red tide of anger. Lifting the hand up across the body. The glorious release, the opening up, the letting out, seeing the boy's sullen face spinning away from your hand.

Wrong, wrong, utterly wrong: to hit a child! But I'm remembering the photo of the school: Connor with his coat a bit awry and those endless little faces lined up in front of a building not big enough for them all. One man, sixty or seventy children. A person can be pushed beyond endurance.

George Huxley deposed: I am nearly 15 years old. I left school last July.

When I attended school Mr Connor used to cane me. He has given me as many as 4 slaps at one time. He caned me once on the head – I think on purpose. He has pulled my ears.

signed, George Huxley

Gertrude Mary Huxley deposed: I am 6 years old. If I am naughty Mr Connor hits me with his hand and pulls my ears. He has never caned me.

Examined by Mr Connor: My mother told me to say that Mr Connor pulled my ears.

Gertrude Mary Huxley, X her mark, witnessed by A.E.

There's six-year-old Gertrude Huxley. Her small face pale with apprehension and the puzzlement of figuring out the right thing to say. Twisting her hands in her pinafore. Her brothers and sisters outside with everyone else waiting to give evidence, and no one with her but Mr Connor and the stranger, Inspector Elliott.

Hard to get a word out of her. *Gertie dear*, Mr Connor says. *You know you must tell the truth, don't you?* Her head down, watching her twisting hands, a jerk of the head that says yes, she knows she has to tell the truth, or at least knows she has to agree with Mr Connor. *Now, Gertie, who told you to say I pulled your ears?* No answer, just the agonised twisting of the little hands, so Connor pulls them away, straightens her dress, leaves the child standing with her hands beside her, the fingers still rubbing and working around each other. *Who told you, Gertie? Hmm? Was it your mother?* A blowfly against the glass, the tall stranger, the Inspector, sitting at the table with his pen in his hand, watching her, waiting, the pen ready to write. Outside a murmuring from all the mothers and pupils, and in a gust of wind the loose shingle on the roof making a *tap tap tapping*. Her eyes going to the door, longing to be walking through it, getting out, getting away, back to the people she knows. The silence is like water drowning her. She nods, a movement of the head hardly made, but enough. The tall man lets out a little breath, a sort of *About time* puff of impatient air, and she hears the scratch of the nib on his paper.

You can go, Gertie, Mr Connor says. *Off you go now.* But Gertie Huxley is still standing there, because something's happened that she hadn't quite meant, the moment had got away from her, her head had nodded because it seemed the only way to stop the silence and get back outside, but now the tall man is writing away and something has swept her up and along to a place she hadn't meant to go.

Deposition by the Defendant, Joseph Connor:

Mr Connor deposed: My name is Joseph Connor. I am 47 years of age and Teacher at the Currabubula Public School. The statement that children are held by the neck and flogged on the back is a deliberate falsehood. If I have to punish a child I punish on the hand. I make a practice of punishing them in this way.

I admit that I caned Lilian Webb about a fortnight ago. She became stubborn and would not answer me. All the school was kept idle for a few minutes and then to annoy me, although good at addition she told me that 18 and 1 make 17. I then gave her two slaps on the hand. There may have been marks after the punishment, but I did not look to see. I only gave ordinary slaps, but the morning was frosty and marks may have been left.

Oh, who needs a novel? *She became stubborn and would not answer me* – I can hear it and see it: the silence of a crowded space with everyone holding their breath, waiting, aghast, a kind of glee. There's Lilian Webb, standing up to give her answer, a pert defiant look on her face, a taunting tone: *Eighteen plus one is seventeen. Sir.* A little rustle around the classroom, sniggers not quite suppressed.

When I was in Grade 4 at North Sydney Demonstration School there was a naughty girl, a wild redhead, Judy Callahan. Fearless, direct, somehow already possessing an adult's conviction that she had the right to be the person she was.

She got into trouble one day and Mrs Linney told her to stay in after school. Whereupon Judy stood up at her desk at the back of the room – I remember the bang of the seat flipping up – and said, loud and clear, "I hate you, Mrs Linney." There was in the room the thick silence I imagine in the Currabubula schoolroom when Lilian Webb *became stubborn*. I turned around to see – we all did – Judy Callahan standing at her desk, her red hair aflame, her hands flat on the desktop, staring at Mrs Linney.

All the class was kept idle for a few minutes.

Mrs Linney didn't have a cane. What she had was the headmistress, Miss Cook. Miss Cook was a person of fearful mystique. Her manner was brisk and brusque but never excited, she never raised her voice or gesticulated. Her stillness was its own dense focused power.

So Judy Callahan lifted the lid of the desk, got out her things, put them in her little Globite case, and in that thick watching silence walked from the back of the classroom past us all, out the door and down to sit outside Miss Cook's office until Miss Cook was ready for her.

Joseph Connor would have caned the children in the classroom, in front of all the other pupils. What a show it would have been – an exhibition, an entertainment, a warning. The mood in the room at North Sydney Demonstration School was the same. We were like every crowd that has ever watched terrible things: excited, mindless, hungry for more.

Remembering that moment with defiant Judy Callahan makes me think again about Connor's account. There's some kind of loose end there, and it's the number Lilian has chosen in order to annoy Mr Connor. *What is eighteen plus one, Lilian?* Defiant Lilian might have been, but would she have come up with the rather elegant, quite subtle bit of mockery of neatly inverting the right answer? I think a cheeky child might say something more ridiculous: *Eighteen plus one makes forty-three, sir*.

Perhaps she simply heard *minus* where Mr Connor said *plus.* So perhaps she wasn't defiant at all, but hard of hearing. Ear infections among children were as common in 1884 as they are now, but before antibiotics they couldn't be treated. Connor's story seems to prove he was right to punish Lilian. The thing is, he doesn't have to be lying to be wrong. He could just be looking at the moment without knowing enough.

> I have not been cruel to Agnes Bradbury, I liked the girl and had great compassion for her after her mother's death. I found her truthful. I can remember caning her but not severely. I have never given her more than 2 slaps at one time.

This sounds right, doesn't it? You'd hesitate to punish a girl of nine or ten who'd just lost her mother. I'm picturing it – the child coming to school in a daze of misery, her mother dying or dead, and Joseph Connor watching with sympathy, seeing the way the other kids don't know how to behave around her, the way she's moving slowly. Noticing the way her once-smooth plaits are lumpy and untidy now that her mother's not there to do them.

Yes. But Bradbury knows the exact date of the caning, *two years ago last October*, because that's when his wife died. He remembers it all too clearly: a time of grief and fear and the dreadful muddle of mourning, and Agnes coming home with the marks on her hand, and he's thinking, How could he, how could that man Connor do this to a child at such a time?

Either Bradbury is lying or Connor is lying. Or is there some way to square those two opposing pictures?

Well, this bit of geometry might do it: Mrs Bradbury is dying, or maybe already dead, but on the day Agnes is punished, Connor hasn't yet heard the news. All he knows is that Agnes is coming to school without having done her homework and she isn't paying attention in class. When he gives the children a piece of long division to do she just sits there staring at her slate, and when he stands over her and puts the chalk in her hand and tells her, *Don't be cheeky, Agnes, do your work*, she doesn't as much as look up at him, just drops the chalk – deliberately! – and pushes the slate off the desk so it falls with a great clatter onto the floor.

> Jane Bradbury, who is said to have received 22 slaps in 4 days, has only received 2 slaps since her first admission to the school.

Connor's got the Punishment Book in his hand. He's leaning over the table, pointing to the entry, two slaps, and turning the pages, showing how Jane Bradbury isn't on any of the others, and Inspector Elliott's beside him, peering at the words and numbers in their tidy columns. Which are, of course, just marks on paper. The only thing you can really know about them is that a human hand has picked up a pen, dipped it in ink, and made certain marks. Beyond that, nothing is sure.

> I very seldom punish Thomas Bradbury, and I do not believe he has been caned once in the last 3 months. My punishment record shows every case of corporal punishment to Mr Bradbury's children. The last date on which Thomas was caned was 24th February 1892; he received 2 slaps for "copying". Thomas is a truthful good boy, and gives no cause for punishment.

I'm starting to listen with a shade of scepticism to what Connor's saying, but I do believe him here. It's something about the awkwardness of *a truthful good boy.* If he'd said *a good truthful boy* it would sound glib. But you can hear his words making their unrehearsed, awkward way along as he describes his inner picture of Thomas Bradbury.

> I deny that the whitlow has been caused by caning received by the boy at school.
>
> With regards to Mr Bradbury's general charge of cruelty I have been in charge here for 6 years under 3 different Inspectors. The other two gave me credit for being hard working and conscientious, and in conversations with you at inspection times you have invariably expressed yourself as being well satisfied with my school work.

This direct address is almost shocking, a kind of breaking of the fourth wall. *You* is Inspector Elliott, of course. He's sitting there at the desk with the pen in his hand and the inkwell in its little hole in the desk, everything orderly and impartial.

But it's not impartial. These two men have a relationship. Elliott is Connor's boss, but he's also his colleague. They're from the same tribe – the tribe of the educated. In 1892 that made them rarities, would have isolated them from their communities. Connor may not have welcomed having his work inspected by Archibald Elliott, but he might have welcomed the chance to spend time now and then with a man he could talk to more or less on the same level. Elliott, living in Tamworth, mightn't be so isolated. But he'd know the clause in the Act that instructed inspectors to be *guided by feelings of sympathy with the labours of the teachers, and treat them with the consideration and kindness which the difficulties of their position demand.*

Connor's taking a risk in making this sudden direct appeal to Elliott, drawing him into the case. But there's also just the shadow of a threat. If the Inspector finds against Connor, it will show that in the past his professional judgement had been wrong.

> Examined by Mr Bradbury: I think this inquiry is the outcome of malice because you were the only person whom Brown could get to sign a petition against me some months ago. More than one person has warned me to beware of you. Your demeanour whenever I have met you in the last 18 months has caused me to think you would injure me if you could.
>
> I came to your house not to apologise concerning Agnes's punishment but simply as a visitor. I think I stayed more than half an hour: we were talking over educational matters. I think I was at your place once before – it was with Mr Dixon, School Attendance Officer.

The question Bradbury must have asked to get this answer must have been something like, *Did you come to my house to apologise for punishing Agnes?* It must have seemed a good question: if Connor came to apologise, it's proof that he did wrong. But far from being trapped, quick-witted Connor sees an opportunity to turn the question to his advantage. He not only denies making an apology, he also uses the moment to let Elliott know that he went to Bradbury's place with the Attendance Officer. What he's saying is, Bradbury has been in trouble for not sending his children to school.

Inspector Elliott writes down the damning detail: *Mr Dixon, School Attendance Officer*. Message received, Mr Connor.

> Examined by the Inspector: I am not positive that my punishment book records every case of corporal punishment inflicted. I am sure that all severe punishments have been recorded and every case of punishment to Mr Bradbury's children has been recorded.
>
> signed, J. Connor
>
> --------
>
> Evidence of Witnesses for the Defendant
>
> Charles Milburne deposed: I am 14 years of age. I have seen Mr Connor cane Thomas Bradbury. I have never seen him get more than 2 slaps at one time. About 7 or 8 weeks ago Thomas showed me a little mark on his right hand. He told me that he had a whitlow. He did not say that the cane caused the whitlow.
>
> Examined by Mr Connor: I have never seen you cane a child on the back. I do not remember being caned.
>
> signed, Charles Milburne

Clifford Morris deposed: I am 13 years old. I attend Currabubula School.

Examined by Mr Connor: I have never seen you take children by the neck and cane them on the back. I know Jane Bradbury. I have never seen her get the cane at school. I know Thomas Bradbury. I do not remember seeing you cane Thomas during the last 3 months. He complained to me that he had a sore finger. He said he had a whitlow but he did not say what caused it. If I were told that you were very cruel to the children, caning them severely over the back, I would not believe it.

signed, Clifford Morris

Barnaby Morris deposed: I am 11 years old.

Examined by Mr Connor: I have never seen you cane a child on the back. If I were told that you were very cruel to the children, caning them severely over the back, I would not believe it. If you took a child by the neck and caned him over the back I would be sure to see it. I am sure nothing of the kind has happened in the school.

I know Jane Bradbury. I remember Jane Bradbury getting the cane about a month ago. I have only seen her caned once & she got 2 cuts.

I remember Thomas Bradbury getting the cane about 4 months ago. I have seen the Clarke boys fighting on their way home from school.

signed, Barnaby Morris

Matthew McCarthy deposed: I am 11 years old.

Examined by Mr Connor: I have never seen you flogging children on the back. I know Jane Bradbury, and I have never seen her caned. I know Thomas Bradbury. I do not remember when you caned him last.

signed, Matthew McCarthy

William Sewell deposed: I am 9 years old.

Examined by Mr Connor: If I were told that you were very cruel to the children, caning them severely over the back, I would not believe it. If you took a child by the neck and caned him over the back I would be sure to see it. I have never seen you take children with the left hand and flog them with the right. I know Jane Bradbury and I have never seen her caned at school. I know Thomas Bradbury. I do not remember him getting the cane.

signed, William Sewell

I've only been cross-examined once in a court of law. I was a character witness for a friend who'd been accused of assaulting her husband. Her cat had scratched him on the arm and he said my friend had done it. As I took the stand and did the declaration thing I was fogged up with fright. Never before and never since have I been so overwhelmed, physically taken over, made incapable by nerves. My hands were cold but sweaty, my mouth dry. All the cliches.

At a great distance I heard myself trotting out the testimony I'd gone through with my friend's barrister. Then the prosecutor got up to cross-examine me. Some easy questions, and then something out of nowhere: What was the cat's name? I felt everyone in the court-room holding their breath and I knew the answer was important, but I didn't know why, because naturally I hadn't been allowed to listen to the rest of the evidence.

I could see the cat, hear it purring, see it on my friend's lap ... but I'd never taken enough notice of what it was called. I felt blood pour into my head as the terrible silence went on. It was like being smothered, and the smothered feeling was from not knowing why it mattered.

I can't remember, I started – my voice a faint croak – but the moment I stopped trying to remember, the name came to me. I just about shouted it: Etchinska! I felt everyone in the courtroom breathe, sit back on their chairs. It was the right answer.

If I was reduced to a jelly when I knew I had nothing to hide and nothing of great significance to contribute, what would those kids have felt?

They all seem to have remarkably poor powers of observation. There's an awful lot they *do not remember*. An awful lot of things they *have not seen*. They have no inclination to put a number on slaps or canings. Hardly surprising. There they are, one by one giving evidence about the teacher they share five days of every week with, Mr Connor eyeball-to-eyeball with them over the desk, firing out his questions about his own behaviour, what he'd done or not done to them and others, in the same way he fires out questions about the twelve times table or the main products of Nottingham, and woebetide if you get it wrong.

Now the classroom has become something like a court of law, the questions different but the same man rapping them out. They'll be sitting in this same room with that man for the next several years. Each one of those kids has thought about that prospect and made the wise choice.

Their answers are so alike, you'd think they've been coached. *If I were told ... I have never seen you ...* But perhaps not. When I put myself in the room, picturing for the first time precisely how the Inspector is recording the event, I realise that he isn't necessarily writing down the exact words being said. He's paraphrasing, summarising, forming nice grammatical sentences out of the clumsy raw matter coming out of the mouths in front of him, and economically combining the question and the answer. It means the words on the page can't be accepted at face value, the way I've been doing.

So, on that cold afternoon in the schoolroom, the Inspector might have asked, *Have you ever seen Mr Connor take children with the left hand and flog them with the right?* Nine-year-old William Sewell, flushed and frozen, dry of throat, sweaty of palm, doesn't quite understand the question, isn't absolutely sure at that moment about right and left, and has to be prompted, *Come on, William, yes or no?* More or less at random he picks what he hopes is the safe answer, a whispered no. Mr Elliott makes his careful note: *I have never seen you take children with the left hand and flog them with the right.*

Sixteen witnesses and a long day in the draughty classroom. Then Inspector Elliott bundles up his pages of notes and goes home to Tamworth to write his report.

28th June 1892
Inspector Elliott to the Chief Inspector

The charges brought against the teacher are six in number. Of these the first and last are indefinite.

The second charge was admitted by the Teacher, who pleaded justification. The child was guilty of bad temper and deserved punishment, but on the day of the enquiry there were two cane marks on the child's hand – nearly two weeks after the caning had been given.

Nothing whatever was given in evidence in support of charge three. Mr Bradbury simply made a statement, and his daughter was not even brought as a witness.

Charge four is the most serious. The boy Thomas Bradbury is suffering from a bad whitlow, and the complaint is that caning caused it. The Teacher's punishment record shows that the boy has not been caned since 24th February – 4 months ago – and several scholars said that the boy had not been caned since that time. The boy himself says that he was caned in April. I am of opinion that the whitlow cannot be attributed to caning.

In charge five the Teacher is said to have given 22 slaps on four successive days to a little child. The evidence goes to show that the child has only received two slaps in twelve months.

The Teacher accuses the complainant of being actuated by malice, stating that Mr Bradbury was the only person who could be got to sign a petition against him 18 months ago. I am satisfied that the Teacher has grounds for his opinion. I learn from outside sources that Mr Bradbury dislikes Mr Connor. The witnesses for the complainant have with one exception all been concerned in previous reports and inquiries against the Teacher.

During the last two years the schools in this district have been under my supervision, and it is only fair to Mr Connor to state that his school is one of the most efficient that I visit.

I recommend:

1. That Mr Connor be informed that although the charges brought against him have not been substantiated, sufficient evidence was advanced at the recent enquiry to show that some of his punishments have been indiscreet, as two children who were examined by the Inspector had cane marks on their hands.

(a) Moreover these enquiries cannot but affect the interests of the school adversely;

(b) and the Minister is therefore of opinion that it will be necessary for Mr Connor when inflicting corporal punishment in future to act with greater discretion and moderation.

2. That Mr Bradbury be informed that the Minister, having considered the evidence taken at the enquiry at Currabubula on 25th June, 1892 and the Inspector's report thereon, is of opinion that the charges brought against the teacher have either been much exaggerated or remain unproved.

A. Elliott

The tiny print runs on smoothly, enumerating, ordering, looking to the one hand and then the other hand, ordering everything into subheads and then subheads of subheads. Inspector Elliott is being seen to do all the right things: hold the enquiry, write it all down, weigh everything up, deliver his judgement. *I am of opinion. I am satisfied. I learn from outside sources.* Elliott doesn't just believe Connor, he pours scorn on Bradbury: *nothing whatever was given in evidence for charge three. His daughter was not even brought as witness.*

The worst Elliott is prepared to say about Connor is that *some of his punishments have been indiscreet.* As far as Inspector Elliott's concerned, Connor's problem is not that he hit the children in his charge. The problem is that he was indiscreet about it. He left *marks.* He got caught.

At high school I was a naughty girl – not a brave one like Judy Callahan, just a grumbling smartypants. In Year 12 I was elected a prefect, but only against the strenuous efforts of the headmistress and her deputy, for whom I represented nothing but trouble.

Once the kerfuffle over me being elected had been resolved, the deputy took the ten of us anointed ones down to the Prefects' Room, our own little privileged space with couches and a kettle and toaster. She issued each of us with a wooden ruler. That was our badge of office, and our official equipment for one of our most important tasks: to police the way the school uniform was worn. Some girls had adapted the uniform to look less daggy, rolling the white socks up and shortening the tunic by hoicking it over the belt. As everyone streamed out the gates in the afternoon, prefects were on duty, rulers in hand. If we spotted any long socks or short skirts we were authorised to stop the wearers and use our ruler to check them. From the ground to the top of the turn-down of the sock was to be not more than 3 inches. The hem was not to be more than 2 inches above the knee. So that we could measure this accurately, the girl was made to kneel on the asphalt.

Instructing us on all this, the deputy head took us into her confidence. You will need to be firm, girls, she said. You might find some of the girls will get upset. There are some silly girls. But just remember: never send them home crying. We don't want the parents up at the school, do we?

We were all uncomfortable. You could feel it in the hot little room, the thought we were all having: was it worth it – the jug and the toaster and the status – to become part of Flo's little army? But none of us said a word.

I have to confess that I stood by the gate with the ruler after school.

I made girls kneel in front of me while I measured the distance of their hem from the ground. I'm deeply ashamed of myself now. But the cringe-making memory tells me a truth about myself that it's probably better to know, and to learn from. I let myself be lured over to the side with the power, rather than standing up for the side that didn't have any. All it takes is seeing something you want. Then you come up with a story that makes it all right to take it. You don't let yourself see the other side of the story, how it feels to kneel on the ground in front of the after-school crowd while another girl measures your skirt.

Connor has to be spoken to, but only to warn him to be more discreet in the future. Figuratively speaking, he's *sent them home crying*.

28th June 1892
John Bradbury to the Minister for Public Instruction

Honourable sir,
Before Inspector Elliott my notice of Inquiry being two Clear days I was unable to have Agnes Bradbury Present who is at a distance.

Honourable sir I being an uneducated man and a Stammerer not being represented by Councel

I procured a ready writer to take Depositions as I am not able to take notes and follow Evidence

Inspector Elliott objected.

Said I should not have them

So my Questions have been at random

In the Evidence Mrs Clarke she stated she had Complained to Inspector Elliott of the illtreatment of her children and had no further Satisfaction in the matter.

The Inspector Admitted as fact but for some Cause left it as it was without Inquiry

in Mrs Huxleys Evidence she had Complained to Police Magistrate and had no satisfaction.

in Answer to Mr Connor did I thrach my son William with a Bullock whip over the head and legs I admitted leaving red marks on his legs but not over the head further Question did I never Strike him over the head. Never over the head. on after reflection remember some months ago in going to Strike on the shoulders with a strap, I struck him on the cheak and left red marks. Thease punishment was for habitual liing.

Many and varyus punishments were inflicet before these harsh measures were resorted to. My entigtry as a Parent I can uphold. Mr Connor has at no Time Complained to me of their bad behaviour. Mr Connor Charges me with Malice by one time Syging a Pition to injure him.

Inspector Elliott charged me with being confedrate with Mr Brown in an Inquiry some 20 months back.

I Positively deny both charges

At Brown Inquiry I wrote to you Stating Mr Connor using the Play ground for yarding his herd of Cattle and of seeing a beast Skined on the grounds. also Stating it would be a benefit to the Pupls a Change of masters. At that time I could have charged him with Cruelty it is in the Evidence of Past Cruelty in Preasent Inquiry.

Inspector Elliott States he has over Site of Schools and grounds. at the Preasent their is a Stable or Cart Shed on the best Part of the ground it being under the Shadow of the Only Tree shading the grounds the grounds are small.That is why we have to make truvl complaints. to my mind and those Preasant Inspector Elliott was Allied with Mr Connor all through the Inquiry in Mrs Clarke complaint refer in Evidence. Mrs Huxley complaining to Police Magistrate show the littel confidence the Parents have in an Inquiry. To my mind any mother brining a Charge would be Browbaton and Hounded off.

In Mr Connor defence he said my charges were a Malicious falshood.

Honorable Minister I bear malice to none.

```
    But I wish to have the benifit of the most liberal
of all Acts of Parlement (Education act.
    And let my Children an Education. the lose of
which I their Parent so keenly feels the need of.
    I Conclude feeling I have worked for the Honour of
the Law and the Prevention of Cruelty.

Respectfully yours
John Bradbury
```

John Bradbury would have been able to read a sky or a paddock or the way a sheep was standing, but he struggles to write a letter. Still, he's making some good points. He only had two clear days' notice of the enquiry – not enough time to gather witnesses. To ride to their houses, scattered across the district, and watch them not knowing where to look as he labours to explain, to plead with the ones who have got the sheep to shear and don't want to lose a day's work. Then back on the horse and on to the next farm. In the city two clear days might have been enough, but not in Currabubula.

Two mothers, on different occasions, have already complained about Connor but they've been *browbaton and hounded off.* His spelling might be eccentric, but what woman among us hasn't been *browbaten and hounded off* by some officious man with no time for a troublemaking female? Calling you *madam* the way men do when they want to cut you down to size, that bogus gallantry that's more insulting than plain rudeness?

And the old business about the playground – it turns out that Connor's shed monopolises the only shade there. That's not something Connor has ever mentioned, and not something Elliott seems ever to have noticed. Not a big deal in itself, you could say, but part of a pattern: omit, mislead, deflect.

And Bradbury's a stammerer! What a corny metaphor for someone who's voiceless. But John Bradbury's stammer is not a metaphor. He's a real man, really suffering. There he is in his farmer's heavy pants, a green stain around the knees, big clumpy boots, his hair cut at home by his oldest girl, longer on one side than the other and in tufts at the back, labouring with his rubbery disobedient mouth that makes every utterance an ordeal.

And there are the other two. Mr Connor, who's prepared his defence, got the children lined up to testify in his favour, assembled as much scuttlebutt about his accusers as he could. Inspector Elliott, that cool, careful man, nicely spoken, nicely educated, in his nice clothes. Well known to Connor, but a stranger to Bradbury. Both of them with the professional gift of the gab. Looking at Bradbury, their smooth faces pretending neutrality. *Do you have any questions for the witness, Mr Bradbury?* So Bradbury feels he has to ask something, but with Connor watching, and Elliott scratching away, and his mind the same blocked muddle that his mouth was, the questions come out as ridiculous. *Are you intimate with me, Mrs Clarke?* With every silly question his brain jamming even more and a great terrible flush coming up into his face.

The cruellest part of the whole thing is that he knows perfectly well what a mess he's making of it. He knows he needs a *ready writer* – someone fluent in the language of reading and writing, who can make notes, assemble an argument, ask the right questions. He'd arrived at the enquiry with that person beside him. But Elliott had stopped him. Oh no, Mr Bradbury, he'd have said, I'm afraid you are not permitted to bring anyone into the enquiry with you. His glasses glittering, catching the light so Bradbury is confronting something not quite human. But I need a ready writer, sir, he tries, cannot do it without.

I'm very sorry, Mr Bradbury, says Elliott, not sounding sorry at all. I can show you – getting out the little booklet, flipping the pages, he knows just where it is – here it is in the regulations. Do you see here, Mr Bradbury? The complainant, the defendant and the witnesses are the only people allowed in the room.

For that, I could hate Archibald Elliott.

It's shame and mortification for Bradbury, and anger, knowing how the whole situation is set up against him. And then the scratching of the damned pen, and the whole complicated story of what happened in the schoolroom with those children, and what was happening now, leaving no trace except those words being laid down forever on the paper by Inspector Elliott's relentless pen.

The Chief Inspector in at Bridge Street must have read John Bradbury's letter with the attention it deserved, and set it alongside Inspector Elliott's report, and formed the view that Mr Inspector needed to explain a few things. The Chief Inspector's letter isn't in the file, but Elliott's response to it is.

1st July 1892
Inspector Elliott to the Chief Inspector

Currabubula: Mr Bradbury's charges against the teacher.

The only matters referred to in Mr Bradbury's present letter not mentioned in either my report or the evidence forwarded are the following:

1. Mr Bradbury brought into the school room a young man who was to take down the evidence of the

the gate before he spots her. Oy, he calls, where do you think you're going? She pretends not to hear, she's up on the horse now, urging it on, along the dusty road, till she gets to the hotel. Goes into the bar, there's George Morris the publican, he's surprised and not best pleased to see her there, a woman in the sacred male space of his quiet bar, flushed and her hair all over the place and a glitter in her eye.

But she's spotted the Inspector, the only man among the few at the bar with shiny shoes. He's embarrassed, cranky, his dignity wounded to be buttonholed by a woman in front of everyone, her voice too loud, while he's in the bar with his pipe and his pint. He tells her to come back the next day, meet him at the school, or put it in writing, madam.

But she can't come back the next day. Can't leave the family again, take the horse again, leave the house with the dinner not done, the baby crying, and the leaden punishing silent disapproval of her husband.

As for putting it in writing, who did he think she was? She was Sarah Clarke from Piallaway. There'd been no school in the district when she was a girl. She could just about sign her name but that was it.

I am satisfied in my own mind of acting with perfect fairness to both sides. But if Elliott was really sure, he wouldn't need to whip himself into a lather of self-righteous indignation. *Either Mr Bradbury should be informed that I enjoy the Minister's confidence; or else another officer should be sent to enquire into Mr Bradbury's charges.* That's an angry man, and his anger is the public face of the secret truth he won't let himself know: he's willing to fudge things to defend Connor.

Malicious Libel

In June 1892, Oscar Wilde hadn't yet sued the Marquess of Queensberry for libel. Hadn't yet been humiliated in court, hadn't spent two years in Reading Gaol. Hadn't fled to Paris and died there making jokes about the wallpaper.

All of that was a few years in the future. Not yet a warning to a person ablaze with indignation.

30th June 1892
Joseph Connor to Inspector Elliott

Sir,
It is my intention to take legal proceedings against Mr John Bradbury for malicious libel in the charges he brought against me, and which were investigated at this school on the 25th instant. This I am willing to do wholly on my own responsibility, and at my own expense, unless the Minister should see fit to prevent my doing so.

Mr Bradbury is evidently under the impression that he may level those charges at me with impunity, but, as this is not his first attempt, I think it is time to undeceive him.

I beg to request, Sir, that Mr Bradbury's charges, as written by himself, together with the written evidence taken at this School on the 25th instant, be given to my Solicitor, R.H. Rose Esq, MLA, whom I have instructed to apply for them at the Department of Public Instruction, Sydney, with a view to institute legal proceedings against Mr Bradbury.

I have the honour to be, Sir, your humble servant,
J. Connor

12th August 1892
John Bradbury to the Minister for Public Instruction

Honorable Sir, feeling that a just and needful complaint has failed through cause or causes unknown to me, and feeling my unfitness to continue leader of those seeking the protection of those children of this locality, I have employed Mr Solicitor Newman Tamworth to act on my behalf. Will you kindly accept him to act in my stead.

Yours respectively
William Bradbury

15th September 1892
The Daily Telegraph, Sydney

Action for Slander

Tamworth, Wednesday – Judge Fitzhardinge presided at the District Court today. An action for slander was brought by the public school teacher of Currabubula, Joseph Connor, against John Bradbury, a selector, to recover 200 pounds damages. It was alleged the defendant had stated that the plaintiff had acted cruelly to the children attending the school and had caused a whitlow to form on the finger of the defendant's son, causing him to lose the use of his digit. Mr R. Thomson, who appeared for the defendant, applied for a nonsuit, and the case was adjourned for decision.

15th September 1892
Inspector Elliott to the Under-Secretary

I return herewith all the papers connected with this case.

I have to report that the verdict was for the Defendant, without costs. The judge when giving this verdict stated that the evidence of malice brought forward by the Plaintiff was insufficient to gain a verdict but he was not satisfied that the Plaintiff's witnesses had stated all they knew. He therefore compromised the matter by making each party pay his own costs.

I have etc.
A. Elliott

Joseph Connor has badly miscalculated. It's not just that he hasn't proved that Bradbury's charges were malicious in intent – the judge has made it embarrassingly clear that the witnesses Connor had brought have let him down. The judge seems to think it's possible they could have proved Connor's case and had chosen not to.

Sensible of them. For the rest of their lives those witnesses, whoever they were, had to go on living with the Bradburys, the Webbs, the Huxleys, the Clarkes. There'd be tendrils of connection that Connor, as an outsider, wouldn't have any idea about – threads linking them from childhood, through marriage, through business, through a favour done last year ... Of course they didn't tell the whole story.

In any case, they mightn't have been on Connor's side. Like me, they might have thought that taking on an uneducated stammerer like Bradbury wasn't something they wanted to be part of. Connor would have sat in court, his face stony as he realised his revenge on Bradbury was backfiring. Even if Connor had won, it would have been an empty victory. Couldn't he have seen that? Imagine walking down the street and having to pretend nothing had happened. Ah, good morning, Mrs Clarke! Nice day, isn't it? and feel your back prickle as you walk on, pretending you didn't care that Mrs Clarke has cut you dead and Mr Gould has just come out of Moorby's shop and is staring too, and if you turned around you'd see them talking behind their hands to each other and Mrs Moorby coming out to join them.

Oh, the humiliation. The high and mighty teacher losing to poor stammering Bradbury with the cow poop on his pants.

The compromise the judge has reached suggests a kind of distaste at what's playing out in front of him: a schoolmaster, a man of relative privilege and power, attacking a man who'd tried to defend his children. From the judge's position up on the bench, Connor might as well have had a sign hanging around his neck: *Bully.*

Accouchement

3rd October 1893
Joseph Connor to Inspector Elliott

Sir,
I have the honour to apply for leave of absence for my wife as teacher of needlework at Currabubula Public School for a period of one month from this date in consequence of her accouchement.
No leave of absence from her duties has been granted to my wife during the past twelve months.

I have etc.
J. Connor

Tristram is Mrs Connor's eleventh *accouchement*.

Some Lung Complaint

19th July 1894

Joseph Connor to Inspector Elliott

Sir,

I regret to say that my wife is at present a patient in Tamworth Hospital, suffering from some lung complaint. The doctor, whose certificate I herewith attach, informs me that my wife is in a very dangerous condition, and that she will not be able to perform any duties for a considerable time.

I therefore humbly request that my wife be exempt from teaching needlework at this school for a period of three months from this date.

I have etc.
J. Connor

18th July 1894

Dr Crisp to Joseph Connor

Mrs Connor is a patient in this hospital suffering from lung trouble and I would recommend that she be granted at least 3 months leave of absence from her duties as Sewing mistress.

Thos. B. Crisp FRCS, Tamworth Hospital

In 1894, if you heard that someone had *some lung complaint* or *lung trouble*, you could be pretty sure they had tuberculosis. But, as for cancer in our times, people were reluctant to give the disease its name. It was dreaded and feared and discussed in euphemisms. It was common, it could strike anyone and it was incurable

And it was contagious. In 1894 people knew that TB was spread by coughing. If the Connors had lived in Sydney, Ann might have been sent to the Coast Hospital on the outskirts of the city, where patients with TB, leprosy, syphilis and smallpox were isolated. You can still see one of the wide-verandahed wards, where TB patients like Mrs Connor were wheeled out in their beds to breathe the clean air coming straight off the Pacific. That was the only treatment doctors could offer. The hospital of a smaller town like Tamworth probably didn't have an isolation ward. Ann would have been sent home with unrealistic instructions to keep away from the rest of the family.

No one would have spelled it out, but everyone would have known that there'd be no getting better for Ann Connor. The little house beside the school at Currabubula would have been a miserable, chaotic place. Ann Connor dying. Joseph Connor humiliated and angry. The new baby – only nine months old – crying on and on. The other children acting out their misery in fighting and tantrums.

For the Department, though, Mrs Connor's illness only had one dimension.

23rd July 1894
Inspector Elliott to Joseph Connor

Currabubula: Absence from duty as Teacher of Sewing of Mrs Connor

Mr Connor: can you arrange for the teaching of needlework during your wife's absence?

A.E.

26th July 1894

Joseph Connor to Inspector Elliott

I have arranged with my housekeeper, Mrs Hazlett, to teach the needlework.

J. Connor

In the world of 1894, when Ann Connor became too sick to go on, the obvious thing would have been for Bridie to resign her teaching post and take over the running of the household. Many a girl of that time was pressured to give up whatever work or training she was doing when the mother of the family was out of action. It was an unusual choice for a family of relatively modest means to employ a paid housekeeper when there was a competent unmarried woman at hand.

But I look again at the photo of Bridie at Terrible Vale. She's happy. To give up her life there and spend her days looking after her mother and the younger children, taking on the backbreaking drudgery of domestic labour – not to mention the teaching of needlework – would be a huge sacrifice.

It would have been hard for her to simply refuse. She'd have been accused of selfishly putting herself before the wellbeing of her family. There'd have been people in the village shocked that she was still riding off every day to Terrible Vale. Her father might have agreed with them that a daughter's first duty was to her family.

Luckily the arithmetic was on her side: a teacher's salary, even at half the male rate, was more than a housekeeper's, so she could stare down the disapproving neighbours. There might have been a residue of guilt, though. Was she abandoning her mother in her hour of need? Was she the unnatural woman that some people already thought her? Was a paid employee really the best person to deal with those little children?

Whatever her wage, Mrs Hazlett earned every penny. She was taking on all the domestic labour Ann Connor had done, but with the extra difficulty of dealing with children distressed by their mother being ill. Unless Ann had been kept in the hospital, Mrs Hazlett was also looking after a woman with an incurable, frightening, contagious illness. All that and the damned needlework as well.

Joseph Connor would have come in every afternoon from the school to a house of crying baby, grizzling children, slowly dying wife and frazzled housekeeper. Still, in among all that, he found time to make yet another enemy in Currabubula.

Not Entertainable

For fourteen years, state education had been secular, free (or nearly free) and compulsory. There'd always been a bit of flexibility about the first two pillars of the new system, but there was no getting around the third. Every child between the ages of six and fourteen had to go to school for the Required Number of Days – roughly two-thirds of the school year. If the roll showed them absent too often without an acceptable excuse, the teacher called in the Attendance Officer, who would visit the parents at home and put pressure on them. If that didn't work, the parents would be taken to court and be made to pay a fine. A second and third offence resulted in heavier fines. In extreme cases a jail term could be imposed.

What stood between the parent and those punishments was the "excuse note", and it was entirely up to the teacher whether or not to accept it.

4th July 1894
Teacher's Special Report on the case of Edwin Watson, father of five children at Currabubula Public School, for breach of the Compulsory Clauses of the Public Instruction Act of 1880, during the half-year ending 30th June 1894.

Name in full: Charles Watson

Age at the end of the half-year: 7 and three-quarters

Name of schools, with attendance at each during the half-year: Singleton 32, Whittingham 8.5, Currabubula 24.5, total 65.

Number of days the school was in operation during the half-year: 107

Distance of nearest school from residence of child: All three not more than a mile.

Parent or guardian: Edwin Watson

Present circumstances: Grazier, appears to be doing well.

Excuse offered for short attendance: Excuses of the most frivolous nature have been offered. The excuses given were too numerous for insertion in so small a space as the tabulated Special Report forms afford. Some of the excuses are: "Mother is ill"; "I had to look after the horses"; "Father sent me on an errand"; "I was ill"; "I had the toothache"; "Mother was afraid it would rain". Mrs Watson informed me that her children were ill on certain dates, whereas on these very dates I saw them going on errands.

Your careful opinion as to the truth and sufficiency of such excuse: Do not believe they were entertainable.

signed, J. Connor

Also

Rosalie: age 11 years 7 months, attended 60 days
Henry: age 13 and a quarter, attendance 62.5
Edward: age 13 and a quarter, attendance 59.5 days
Daisy: age 7 years, attended 63.5 days

You can hear Connor's anger in the prim language: *excuses of the most frivolous nature*, and in the heavy wit about the form not being big enough to contain them all.

It sounds as if he's right to be angry. The children were only at school for sixty-five out of 107 days – absent almost as often as they were present. Some of the excuses do sound of the "dog ate my homework" variety. *Mother was afraid it would rain.* Oh, poor diddums might get wet!

29th September 1894
Tamworth Advertiser

School Attendance Case: An Indignant Parent

Edwin Watson, Currabubula, was summoned for not sending his five children to school the required number of times for the half-year ending 30th June last.

The cases were taken separately.

In the case of Charles Watson, which was taken first, defendant pleaded not guilty.

Joseph Connor, teacher at the Currabubula Public School, stated that the school was open on 107 days during the half-year and the attendance of the child in question was 65. The Act provided the minimum attendance at 70 days. During the half-year mentioned the boy attended three schools, his attendance being as follows: Currabubula PS 21 1/2 days; Singleton PS, 32 days; Whittingham PS 8 1/2 days; these added together made a total of 65 days' attendance during the half year. The boy was enrolled at the Currabubula PS on 30th April last.

In answer to the defendant's question, Mr Connor stated: I am aware that there has been a lot of sickness in the district and the Currabubula Creek has on several occasions been impassable: in 7 or 8 days it would have been impossible for your children to get across.

Defendant: It is very hard to bring me here when the boy comes within 5 days of the prescribed time.

In answer to Sergeant Gamble the teacher stated that no excuse was offered for non-attendance of the children until the end of the half-year.

The Police Magistrate inflicted a fine of 1s, and 4s 10d costs; in default 48 hours' imprisonment.

In the case of his daughter Daisy, defendant pleaded not guilty and similar evidence was given.

The Police Magistrate imposed a penalty similar to that in the previous case.

Defendant (addressing the teacher): This is a shameful case. I'll report you to headquarters.

Teacher: I can't help that. I'm only doing my duty.

Defendant: It is very hard to bring me, a poor hardworking man, here, especially when I come within five days of the time allowed. The children had influenza and the creeks were up and they could not get across. I'll report you to the Department.

Sergeant Gamble: Mr Connor is only doing his duty.

Defendant: Doing his duty! He's exceeding it by a long way. I'll report him for it.

Police Magistrate: Will you be quiet?

Defendant: It's a shameful case and —

Police Magistrate: If you don't keep quiet I'll put you somewhere where you will.

The third case was called on and defendant said that as they were all alike he would plead guilty.

Fines similar to those inflicted in the preceding cases were imposed.

Defendant said he had no change but would give his cheque for the amount.

The Court Penalty Sergeant explained that he was not allowed to take cheques in payment of fines and the Sergeant said he would send to the Bank for the money.

Defendant then sat down at the table to write out his cheque when the teacher came and whispered to him that he would lend him the money until he went to the Bank.

Defendant (scornfully): I don't want your money; I've got my own.

Defendant then wrote out a cheque for the amount and handed it to the Sergeant, who sent it up to the Bank.

Defendant was detained until the cheque was cashed, which was only a matter of a few minutes.

Connor had constructed what looked like an unanswerable argument. I was convinced. So was the Department. But he didn't have to tell any lies for the story to be wrong. He only had to fail to mention a couple of things.

In his report to the Department, Connor had said that the children were only at school for sixty-five out of 107 days, which was true. But the Required Number of Days in that particular half-year (allowing for holidays and other non-school days) was seventy. As Watson points out, the children were only short by five days. And in that same half-year, the Watson family had moved twice, the second time from a town a couple of days' travel away.

Connor says that *no excuse* was given for the missing five days, but that's simply not true. There *were* excuse notes – it's just that Connor had dismissed them as *not entertainable*. But when Watson challenges him, he has to admit that when the children missed those few days of school, *there had been a lot of sickness in the district*. He had to agree that *the creek had been on several occasions impassable*. So Mrs Watson thinking it *looked like rain* isn't as frivolous as it might sound: a child sent to school in the morning could be caught on the wrong side of the swollen creek by the afternoon.

Watson has to pay up because, strictly speaking, he's guilty. But it's hard to read the reporter's account without agreeing with Watson (and with the reporter, I suspect) that it's a *shameful case*.

That's a weird moment at the end of the hearing, when Connor offers to lend Watson the money. Perhaps he's making a show of generosity to try to mend fences. A bit late in the day for that! Or was it one last jab at Watson, intended to humiliate? Watson certainly took it that way.

Frankly, what was Connor thinking, setting all this in train when he could have just accepted the excuse notes? A kindly response might be that things were so bad at home that his judgement was skewed. A man under unbearable pressure within his own family might lash out at another man and his family, unconsciously trying to ease the pain by sending it outwards. Still, what a man does under pressure reveals some fundamentals about the way he's made.

In any case, he picked the wrong mark here. Edwin Watson is no semi-literate stammerer.

1st October 1894
Edwin Watson to the Minister for Public Instruction

Sir,
I wish to call your attention to a very hard case. On the 29th of last month I was summoned to Tamworth, a distance of over 25 miles, for the non-attendance of my children at the Public School, Currabubula. Some of the children were three days short, some Five. I clearly proved that the Children had been prevented through flooded state of creeks and sickness. The teacher also admitted he knew the creek had been uncrossable a good many times.

I may mention this teacher has been here about ten years and from the short time I have been here I can truthfully state I never heard of a worse conducted school. The poor Class of People seem to be in terror of this Teacher and a great Many of the parents have told me they would never send their children only they are compelled by the Act. I am told by the people it's quite useless to appeal to the Inspector here as he is a particular friend.

The children from the Smallest to the biggest have not slightest Respect for this man. I do not wish to injure this man in any way. I only Ask if it is in your powers to get a removal.

Trusting you will give this your consideration,

I remain, yours obediently,
E. Watson

Back at the start of all this, when I was trying to work out why Joseph Connor was being attacked, I thought it might be because he was the visible face of a newly intrusive government. Here, at last, that idea is finally spelled out for the first time – *only compelled by the Act*. I suppose I could take it as confirmation that yes, this is a story about people pushing back against Big Government, but that doesn't feel right.

Certainly the compulsion *was* resented by some, just as there was probably some truth to the idea of *sectarian animosity* lying behind Joseph Connor's troubles. But too much else has happened. There've been too many complaints that sound legitimate, and too many times when Connor's been slippery with the truth. I'd like to know why things happened the way they did. But falling back on an answer as simple as resistance to government intrusion would be bending this file out of shape.

15th October 1894
Inspector Elliott to Edwin Watson

Dear Sir, I shall be glad to meet you at Currabubula PS at 9 o'clock on Thursday morning to enquire into your charges against the teacher, Mr Connor.

Yours faithfully,
A. Elliott

Now this is awkward. Edwin Watson hasn't written to the Inspector. He's bypassed him and gone right to the top, to the Minister. He's done that because he thinks the Inspector is *a particular friend* of Joseph Connor. It's not the first time someone has suggested that.

But the Minister has handed the problem right back to that *particular friend.* The only recourse offered to Watson is to have a personal meeting with him. The meeting will be at the school, on a school day, so Connor will be part of it. It's an ambush.

A week later Elliott summarises the conflict for the Department, praising Connor as *a hard working and efficient public servant.* A postscript adds that *I visited Currabubula on 18th inst and asked Mr Watson to meet me at the school so that I could enquire into his charges against the teacher, but Mr Watson failed to attend.*

Joseph Connor one, Edwin Watson nil.

8th October 1894
A.W. Brown to the Minister for Education

Sir,
At the request of a few residents, I take the liberty to ask your consideration of a few remarks I am about to make with reference to the case, Mr Connor, Teacher, versus Mr Watson for not sending five of his children

the required number of days, which was recently tried at the Tamworth Police Court, and resulted in Mr Watson having to pay the penalty and costs.

Now, Sir, taking into consideration the unfortunate and adverse circumstances that were against Mr Watson since the beginning of this year, viz, having to shift his place of residence twice at great cost and trouble; secondly the frequent uncrossable state of the Currabubula creek; and thirdly, the prevalence of the influenza epidemic, I feel justified in saying it is shamefully tyrannical to take such harsh steps against an unfortunate parent. And I feel assured, that when this is brought under your notice you will not tolerate it one moment.

We have had already too much Court work in connection with this school. Some short time ago Mr J. Bradbury, because he had written to the Department complaining of the cruelty and severity of the Teacher to his children, was actioned by the Teacher for lible, and although a verdict was given in favour of the defendant without costs – that his children were cruelly treated he was not compensated one penny.

Again, Msrs J. Bradbury and A. Gould were prosecuted because there children were from two to three days behind time, and, despite the fact that one of the parents had just came home from a lengthy confinement in the Maitland Hospital, they were fined without being allowed to defend themselves.

If the Department desires to compel parents to send their children to school the required number of days it ought also compel the teacher to keep the yards clean and not allow the teacher to build pigsties and breed cattle on the play ground, as was the case at this school when a report was sent into the Department against the same. The residence yard, in which is the under ground tank, is used for a cattleyard.

It is time we have had pease and freedom from such shameful Police Courts proceedings which only give rise to hatred and illfeeling and cause parents to send there children elsewhere.

I presume Mr Watson has brought this matter under your notice; if so, I hope you will take the contents of my letter into consideration with Mr Watson's.

I believe the removal of the present Teacher will be to the satisfaction of those who are opposed to him. I will now leave this question for your deliberation and hope you will decide to remove the present Teacher and thus end further trouble.

I am, sir, Your obedient Servant,
A.W. Brown

I can imagine the eye-rolling at the Department when Brown comes back, yet again, to the business of the cattle on the playground. But what strikes me here is something the file is otherwise silent about – the little throwaway line about Bradbury and Gould also being prosecuted for not sending their children to school on the Required Number of Days, and by the same slim margin as Watson's children. If this is true, I can only say, you fool, Joseph Connor. You stiff-necked self-righteous arrogant fool.

Shameful

There's a sense of things accelerating, of people massing against Connor. And now the trouble also involves his son Alfred. He's seventeen years old and the pupil-teacher at Currabubula. He takes his class in a weather-shed attached to the main schoolroom that's recently been boarded in and provided with a glass partition to make an improvised second classroom.

15th October 1894
From Margaret Kelly to the Minister for Public Education

Sir,
I am sorry to trouble you but have had reason to complain several times to the school master here of the way he has ill-used my children he seems to take no notice whatever my eldest boy I have removed to another school and now the assistant teacher his son has been ill-using one of my little girls as the child is delicate and if this treatment is continuing I shall be forced to keep her at home I consider as poor people being forced to send our children to school we should be provided with a proper teacher, the way this school is conducted is shameful.

I remain
Your obedient servant
Mrs C. Kelly

Mrs Kelly's indignation would be more convincing if it wasn't that Joseph Connor had chased the Kellys for non-payment of school fees two years earlier. Margaret's husband, Christopher, had been on the receiving end of Connor's little spurt of anger, that snide comment about Kelly feeling *he should always be exempt.*

And here we go again, for the fourth time in four years: another enquiry, with the Inspector sitting at the table at the front of the schoolroom, pen in hand, Mr Connor in the other chair with a look of lofty unconcern on his face, Mrs Kelly sitting pointedly turned away from them, and a stream of witnesses through the quiet room.

27th October 1894
Inspector Elliott to the Chief Inspector

Currabubula: Mrs Kelly's complaint against Mr J. Connor and Master A. Connor, teachers.

Evidence of the complainants, Mrs Kelly and Christopher Kelly Jnr:

Mrs Kelly stated:

My name is Margaret Kelly, and my husband is a labourer. Four years ago I had to complain to Mr Connor for hitting my boy in the face with the back of his hand. He had a black eye for 3 months.

There's no mention of a ring, but the picture is the same as Abner Clarke in the earlier enquiry. That backhand slap across a child's face.

Twelve months ago my husband wrote a letter to Mr Connor complaining of the way he treated my boy and girl. Eleven weeks ago I took my boy from the school, because the Teacher had given him 8 cuts on the hand, and after refusing to hold his hand out for more he was marked over the legs. The boy was pushed against something hard and a lump, which stayed on his neck for 3 weeks, was raised. The boy has been marked on many other occasions.

Four weeks ago, the pupil-teacher caught my little girl by the neck and shook her, and when she nearly fell, he caught her by the throat. She began to vomit, and the pupil-teacher told her not to vomit in School, but to go outside. Her pinafore was all marked from the vomiting.

She's got specifics: the dates, the number of punishments, and the kind of detail you mightn't invent, in language that sounds authentic and unrehearsed. *Her pinafore was all marked from the vomiting.*

But Connor has a line of questioning up his sleeve that casts doubt on everything she says.

Examined by Mr Connor: I did not write the letter myself. I work at Mr Watson's place one day in the week. I had no conversation with either Mr or Mrs Watson over these complaints. I took the boy from school 11 weeks ago. I did not report the matter at that time because I did not intend taking action. It was the pupil-teacher's treatment of my girl that caused me to report at all. I came to you 3 years ago suffering from diphtheria, or from an ulcerated throat. You treated me, but I consider that I cured myself. I have owed you for copybooks and exercise books, but that has nothing to do with the present complaint.

signed, M. Kelly

As he's done in earlier enquiries, Connor sets out to discredit the witness rather than address her accusations. He establishes a very damning fact: she works *at Mr Watson's place*. Inspector Elliott won't have forgotten that Watson would bear Connor a grudge after the business of the *Required Number of Days*. The Inspector will draw the obvious conclusion: Watson has pressured Mrs Kelly to make the complaint, perhaps even written the letter for her. Mrs Kelly might deny having any conversation with Watson about it, but isn't that unlikely?

Just in case that's not enough, Connor then establishes Mrs Kelly's poor character. She'd turned to him – as the man of education in the village – for advice about her sore throat, yet here she is, ungratefully complaining about him. And she's owed him money for schoolbooks. Mrs Kelly may not be educated, but she can see exactly what he's doing. She pushes back: *that has nothing to do with the present complaint.*

Connor's working hard to show Mrs Kelly in a bad light. The one thing he doesn't do is prove her wrong about him mistreating her children.

> Evidence of witness for the complainant:
> Christopher Kelly stated: I am 12 years of age. I was taken away from School some weeks ago because Mr Connor caned me too much. The most slaps that I have had at one time were 4, but one day I got during that day 14 slaps on the hand. I got the cane for answering wrongly.
>
> Examined by Mr Connor: The pupil-teacher ordered me into School for calling him Alf. He ordered me into school twice. I came in once, but refused the second time. I do not remember being sent in for swearing or for beating a little boy. I have never been fighting on

the way home from school. I remember being kept in for history. While I was kept in I refused to look at the book. I do not remember giving you any back answers.

signed, Christopher Kelly

Faced with this barrage of accusations masquerading as questions, all Christopher Kelly can do is retreat to the feeble *I do not remember*.

Evidence of the Defendants, Joseph Connor and Alfred Connor:

Mr Connor states: The boy was last punished by me on 14th June, '94. He got 2 cuts on the hand for inattention. On 7th June he received 2 slaps for neglect. On 6th June he received two slaps for disobedience. This was the occasion when he declined to come into school. The only occasion on which he got 4 slaps this year was on 26th Feb. He got this punishment for disobedience.

It was quite common for the pupil-teacher to complain of him using bad language in the playground. He has been in the habit of striking little boys, not a boy of his own size. On one occasion I punished him on the seat because he refused to hold out his hand.

signed, J. Connor

Master Connor stated: My name is Alfred Connor. I am 17 years of age and I am a pupil-teacher at Currabubula Public School.
Examined by the Inspector: I know Sarah Agnes Kelly. She is generally a well-conducted child. I have to send her for the cane sometimes for neglecting work. I think the greatest punishment she has received was 2 slaps on the hand. I have had to punish her by keeping

her in. A few times I have caught hold of her arms to bring her on to the floor. I have never caught her by the neck or throat.

Alfred's painting a nasty picture here, and it's all the worse for the fact that he doesn't seem to see the nastiness. Sarah Kelly, nine years old, has to be sent to be caned, kept in after school and wrestled to the floor. If a *generally well-conducted child* gets that treatment, what do the poorly conducted ones get?

I do not remember her being sick in the schoolroom. One day about 2 months ago she asked me to go out. She looked pale.

Would he really remember something so insignificant, two months later?

When on playground duty I have frequently ordered Christopher Kelly in school for hurting small boys, using bad language, and playing forbidden games. He always refused to go into school, excepting on one occasion.

I deny that I ever hit a child about the head or body either with my hand or a stick. I send them to my father for punishment.

Examined by Mrs Kelly: I do not remember catching your little girl by the neck and choking her and then catching her by the throat. I do not remember telling her to go outside to be sick.

Oh, his memory's good enough to remember a child asking to go out two months before, but it suddenly fades when Mrs Kelly tries to pin him down. He doesn't deny what she's accusing him of. Caution, or some halfhearted honesty, makes him fall back on the same defence as Christopher Kelly. He *does not remember* choking Sarah. He *does not remember* making her go outside to be sick.

> Examined by Mr Connor: You have told me that no person but yourself was to correct children. When Christopher Kelly had disobeyed me several times you were compelled to take sole supervision of the playground chiefly on account of the boy Kelly's conduct. I can see you through the glass partition all day long. It would be impossible for you to give a child 14 slaps without my seeing.
>
> signed, A. Connor

To my ear this sounds like a well-rehearsed little dance of praise. The detail of the glass partition is a nice touch.

> Evidence of Witnesses for the Defence:
>
> William Sewell stated: I am 11 years old.
>
> Examined by Mr Connor: I know Christy Kelly. I have seen him disobey the pupil-teacher in the playground. I have heard him using bad words. I have heard him giving you back answers. I have seen him kept in for not preparing lessons, and he has refused to look at the book after he was kept in. The most slaps I have ever seen him get at one time was 4. I have never seen him get more than 6 in one day.
>
> Examined by the Inspector: I have never seen Mr Connor hit him on the head with his hand. I have never seen Master Connor punish Sarah Kelly, and I have never heard of her being sick in the schoolroom.
>
> signed, William Sewell

Katie McCarthy stated: I am 15 years old.

Examined by Mr Connor: I have heard Christy Kelly give you insolence. He muttered, and refused to hold out his hand for punishment. I have never seen him get more than 4 slaps at one time. I have never seen you hit him on the legs or back with a cane or thump him about the head.

Examined by the Inspector: I have never seen Master Connor hit Sarah Agnes Kelly. I have seen her sent to Mr Connor for punishment.

About a month ago she was sick in the schoolroom. She did not say that Master Connor had caused her sickness.

signed, Katie McCarthy

Barnaby Morris stated: I am 14 years old.

Examined by Mr Connor: I remember Christopher Kelly disobeying the pupil-teacher in the playground on several occasions. I have seen him disobey you in school. I have seen him refuse to hold out his hand for punishment and I have heard him giving you insolence.

signed, Barnaby Morris

Connor's questions produce a relentless stream of details about what a terrible boy Christopher Kelly is. And there's Elliott sitting at the table, dipping the pen in the inkwell, scraping the excess ink off on the side so it doesn't blob, writing away, glancing up at the witnesses, bending back to his page, and never lifting his head to say, *Mr Connor, I must remind you that it is not Christopher Kelly's behaviour being examined here, but yours.*

Like the kids, the adults have been carefully chosen by Connor to support him.

George Morris stated: I am 41 years of age, and I am the proprietor of the hotel.

Examined by Mr Connor: My boys have attended your school for 10 years. I am quite satisfied with the way you have instructed my boys. I have asked you not to be hard on Cliff because he was sickly. I remember you telling me that you would not punish him at all. I have had to complain of Christopher Kelly's conduct. He is rude in his manner, and on one occasion I had to chastise him for calling me Morry.

signed, George Morris

George Morris is the owner of the Morris Hotel and several other businesses in the town, an educated and prosperous man. Joseph Connor will have wanted to keep on his good side. Of course he'd agreed to go easy on sickly Cliff.

When Mrs Kelly took her son away from Currabubula she sent him to the only other school within walking distance of Piallaway: Terrible Vale, where Bridie has now been in charge for four years. Connor has called her as a witness.

Bridget Connor stated: I am 20 years old, and I am the Teacher of Terrible Vale Provisional School. The Teacher at Currabubula is my father.

Examined by Mr Connor: Christopher Kelly is one of my pupils. In the playground he has caused more trouble than any other pupil and he is the cause of my pupils misbehaving themselves more than they did formerly. He has introduced smoking among them, brings tobacco and makes cigarettes and Albert Whyman has been seriously ill from the effects of eating tobacco given to him by Christy Kelly. Albert is only 4 years old. He also has used filthy language to my pupils in the playground. Some of the girls' sisters have told me of it. I caned him last Wednesday. He told the children I could not hurt him but my father could. He played the truant yesterday. He has been inclined to give me insolence. He will do little homework – a little writing, but no preparation.

Examined by Mrs Kelly: I do not know where he got the tobacco from.

signed, B. Connor

Bridie's account is full of vivid, specific, credible details. Christy Kelly gets the other children to smoke, he poisons a four-year-old with tobacco, he truants, he refuses to do his work, he's insolent, he mocks her and he uses language that's not just bad but *filthy*.

I imagine her: not a big woman, but standing very straight, speaking up confidently. Authoritative, convincing, a reliable witness. She and her father would have gone over the points she's going to make. Connor has only to lead her through them one by one. She's telling the truth, and even letting herself momentarily get vehement with that word *filthy*.

As an intelligent woman she must have known that she had nothing relevant to add to the case. But Joseph Connor is her father. How could she not help him when he asks?

Mrs Kelly – probably unprepared to hear this deluge of bad things about her son – is finally snookered. All she can think of to ask is a weak and pointless question: where Bridie thinks Christopher got the tobacco. She's probably trying to make a case for it being impossible for him to have accessed tobacco, but it's a feeble effort. Even the most determined mother can be out-manoeuvred.

One day I picked my daughter up from primary school and asked her what they'd all been doing in class. I could see her re-running the day in her six- or seven-year-old mind. Finally she said, We waited for Ashleigh to be quiet.

Ashleigh was restless, noisy, aggressive. Couldn't sit still. Couldn't pay attention. Lashed out at the teacher, at other children. Then he was diagnosed with ADHD and dyslexia. He was medicated, and he was no longer disruptive.

It's more than possible that Christy Kelly was like Ashleigh. What torture for such a child to be faced with a book, and then as punishment made to stay in after school and read another book. But like Ashleigh, he was lucky enough to have a mother prepared to stick up for him.

Most of the evidence in this entire enquiry has been about what a terrible boy Christy Kelly is. But he's not the one on trial here. The question isn't whether Christy Kelly is a bad egg, but whether Joseph Connor hits him more than he's allowed to.

31st October 1894
Inspector Elliott to the Chief Inspector

Currabubula: Mrs Kelly's complaint against the Teacher and Pupil-Teacher

The evidence of Mrs Kelly and her son is to the effect that Christopher Kelly has on several occasions been beaten by Mr Connor, and that these beatings have not been confined to the hands. No witnesses were brought forward in support of the statements made.

On the other hand the evidence of Mr Connor, supported by that of several witnesses, shows that the boy has never been severely punished. He appears to have never received more than 4 slaps at one time, and all his punishments, excepting in one instance, have been on the hand. He was once punished on the seat, because he defied the Teacher and refused to hold out his hand.

Regarding the charge against the Pupil-Teacher, Mrs Kelly stated that Master Connor had on one occasion caught her little girl by the throat and shaken her. No witness proved this charge, and the child was not brought to the enquiry, so that I had no opportunity of questioning her. The Pupil-Teacher gave the charge an emphatic denial. He confessed however that he had occasionally caught hold of the child's arm to get her on to the floor when she was misbehaving.

Mr Connor stated that the Punishment Book contained every case of corporal punishment inflicted in his room; but the Pupil-Teacher does not appear to have been sufficiently particular with his entries.

Several charges have during the last 4 years been made against this Teacher, but none of them have been proved. He appears to have a few enemies, but the bulk of the residents are well satisfied with his work. I have made several inspections of the school, and I have always found it in a very satisfactory condition. I regard the Teacher as a painstaking, industrious and efficient officer.

It is not a wise arrangement to have the Teacher's son as a Pupil-Teacher in the same school, and as it would be in the interest of both the school and the Pupil-Teacher to have a change, I shall take the first opportunity that offers of recommending his removal.

A. Elliott

There's something uncertain about Inspector Elliott's verdict here. He's not quite as sure of Connor's innocence as he was last time. On every point, all he's willing to say is that the charges were *not proved*, or that *no witnesses were brought forward to support them.* Connor's behaviour only *appears* blameless, and that's only *according to the Punishment Book.* Like me, Inspector Elliott isn't quite sure what's going on at Currabubula Public School. I think I'm hearing the distant rustle of a man covering his own backside.

A Painfully Sad Story

March 22nd 1895
The Armidale Express

The Raleigh Sun says: – On Monday last Mrs Frederick Street (née Mary White), of Gleniffer, left for Currabubula to see her sister, Mrs Connor, who is said to be dying of consumption. Mrs Connor's husband, who is a public school teacher, is in hospital suffering from a dangerous attack of the pleurisy. One of the children, a boy, is laid up with a broken shoulder, and another boy is suffering with a broken leg. It is a painfully sad story, and the unfortunate family will have the sympathy of everyone who feels for those in distress.

You have to hope Ann Connor didn't read in the newspaper that she was *said to be dying*. It's not something you want to share with every stranger. She'd probably have known, though, and at that point in her illness, death might not have held too many terrors. But she'd be grieving for the children who were about to lose their mother.

And her husband is now in the hospital. *A dangerous attack of the pleurisy* could be a dangerous attack of pleurisy, unpleasant but transient. But Dr Crisp would have known that a teacher diagnosed with tuberculosis – incurable and infectious – would be out of a job. The symptoms are similar enough. Better for the sake of the man and his family to call it pleurisy. And, as if some curse had fallen on the Connors, two of the Connor boys are injured.

A week after this blunt piece in the paper, Ann Connor was dead. She was forty-five, a woman who'd never had a chance at being anything but a domestic drudge and a baby-making machine. Twenty-three years of babies crying and toddlers whingeing and older children squabbling. Year after year of washing cloth nappies, by hand, with water lugged in a bucket from the pump. Before one lot was washed and dried and folded, there'd be another smelly bucketful. There'd never have been a moment when she could stand back and say, There! All done! Imagine if she'd had a musician's spirit, or an engineer's, or a doctor's. Or if she'd simply wanted now and then to have a day off, or an afternoon to walk out and smell the roses.

Did she enjoy her babies, or was she too worn out to be able to laugh? Was she cranky, nagging away at Joseph and the children? Or did she trudge in silence through every endless day, nodding tiredly as her husband exploded yet again in outrage about Arthur Brown, or John Bradbury, or Edwin Watson, or Mrs Clarke, or Mrs Webb, or Mrs Huxley, or Mrs Kelly – the conspiracy against him, an innocent hardworking man?

All that's lost now, impossible to know. What I can see, though, is Ann Connor looking at her boys, one on crutches with his leg in a great heavy plaster, the other with his arm in a sling. They'd get better. Still, to leave them all was heartbreaking. Tristram was only eighteen months old. He'd have no memory of her. For Beatrice she'd be the faintest of memories. For the boys with broken bones, her death and their own pain would be forever mixed up into a blur of misery.

I'm thinking about those boys and their broken bones. Of course this was a world full of accidents waiting to happen. Axes and horses and guns as well as all the usual incidents of boys falling out of trees. It's perfectly possible that two children could have broken bones at the same time. Still, there are all those accusations. All those other children *hit* and *marked*.

And Joseph Connor – what did he feel about his wife's death? He'd been married to Ann Connor for twenty-three years, in the bed with her for just about every one of those nights. I know him much less than when I started, when I had such a vivid and unshadowed picture of him. All I can see now, when I think of him, is darkness and doubt.

Better Removed at Once

When I'd done that second trip to the Archives I'd conscientiously photographed the file for Terrible Vale Provisional School. On a quick flip-through that day, the file had looked a dull little thing, with nothing more than a few exchanges about a measles epidemic and the need for a water tank. It's only now, puzzling away about Joseph Connor and coming to no conclusions, that I read every page. Beyond the letters about spouting and guttering there's this:

> **11th July 1896**
> Joseph Connor to Inspector Elliott
>
> Sir, I hereby request that my daughter be removed from Terrible Vale Provisional School.
>
> She has left her home and is boarding at a public house, and I have reason to believe that she would be better removed at once.
>
> I have etc.
> J. Connor

At first I think I must be misreading the old handwriting. Or that it's about someone else, or there's been some kind of mix-up. It takes me a long confused time before I can believe it's saying what it is. Bridie Connor has *left her home and is boarding at a public house.*

There was only one pub in Currabubula: the Morris Hotel. It was an orderly and respectable house, but in 1896 any hotel was a male domain. A woman accompanied by her husband or brother might take a room for a few nights, but only a certain kind of unaccompanied woman would *board* in a hotel. For a female teacher to do so was more than unconventional. It was shocking, impossible. For the sensible, competent, good-girl Bridie I've imagined, it seems absurd. And this isn't a walk-out-in-a-huff-and-come-back-the-next-day thing. *Boarding* is long term.

Joseph Connor says *I have reason to believe that she would be better removed at once.* That form of words suggests that there's a particular *reason to believe.* The most obvious, I suppose, is that Bridie's fallen for someone her father doesn't approve of: a Protestant, perhaps, or a Jew, or an Aboriginal man, or a person Joseph Connor might have referred to as a *Celestial.* Or someone too young or too old, or the wrong social class, or a smooth-tongued cad who couldn't be trusted with a young virgin. Or, unthinkable in those days, a woman.

Bridie is twenty-one. She doesn't need her father's permission to marry, no matter what he thinks of her heart's desire. But marriage doesn't seem to be an option here. Perhaps the man is already married. Or perhaps he's a cad who's stolen her heart and now dumped her. Or maybe *he* is *she.*

I have reason to believe. Stories multiply in my mind, some more dramatic than others, to explain that choice of words. All possible, all plausible.

Over my dead body! Joseph Connor is shouting. Then you've lost your daughter! she's shouting back. She storms into the bedroom and throws some things into a carpet bag, all the brothers and sisters goggling from the doorway. Good riddance to you! her father bellows as she sweeps out of the house, crosses the road and strides the hundred yards to the Morris Hotel. She works something out with George Morris and goes upstairs to one of the rooms.

Bridie would have known that boarding at the hotel wasn't going to work for long. If she'd had time, she'd have been able to work out something better. She might have found lodgings with a family – Miss Short had boarded with the Moorbys. Or she could have found a respectable boarding house in the bigger town of Werris Creek. Or she could have applied for a transfer to another school. But whatever's happened here was sudden. There's been a crisis. Emotions boiling up past bearing. And once Archibald Elliott reads that letter he's obliged to act quickly. There's no time for Bridie to come up with a more workable plan.

But even as she's explaining to George Morris, asking for a room – how exactly would that conversation have gone? – she'd know that she's handed her father a weapon he can use against her.

Hungrily, hastily, I turn through the next pages of the file, in a frenzy to find out what happened.

17th July 1896
Inspector Elliott to the Chief Inspector

Since Mrs Connor's death the relations between Mr Connor and his daughter have become so strained, that the latter has left her home. She cannot obtain

board near the school and is compelled to stay at the Currabubula hotel – four miles from the school. As I think it desirable for the sake of all concerned that a change should be made, I have to recommend that Mr Uriah B. Burgess be appointed teacher of Terrible Vale Provisional School and that Bridget Connor replace him as teacher of Mullaley Provisional School.

A. Elliott

I think Archibald Elliott knew why things had become *strained*. But he's not going to say – not in a letter to the Department, and therefore not to a stickybeak a hundred and fifty years later. I pore over the few words in his letter, looking for a loose end I can pull at. There are the words, clear on the page in Inspector Elliott's neat tiny script. What he *writes* is clear enough. But what he *knows* is hidden. The words are impenetrable: smooth, tight, painfully neutral.

Or are they? That word *compelled* jumps out at me again. She is *compelled* to stay at the hotel, just as she was *compelled* to go on living at home. She's doing that because *she cannot obtain board near the school.* Is Inspector Elliott telling his superiors not to blame Miss Connor? That she's not a loose woman choosing to live at the pub, but a person in an intolerable situation who doesn't have any other choice? And that phrase, *I have to recommend* – do I hear reluctance, as in *I am forced to recommend*? Certainly he doesn't have many options. Sending Bridie to another school appears to be the only way to resolve the problem.

When he says the strained relations are *since Mrs Connor's death*, is that a clue to what's happened? Perhaps the blow-up wasn't the novelettish story of forbidden love at all, but something to do with the changed dynamics in that house beside the school. With one parent gone, the little universe of that family would have rearranged itself.

After a death there can be recriminations. A daughter blaming a father for not being kinder to a sick wife, perhaps. Connor glances in the door after his day's work. How are you feeling, dear? But doesn't go into the room, doesn't sit with her as Bridie is doing, holding her hand and stroking the hair from her forehead. Doesn't bring the unwanted cups of tea, the unwanted scones, the unwanted chicken broth, to try to tempt the invalid. It's Bridie who does all that. Joseph, that chilly man of no softness, has done none of it.

Or *does* he sit with her, try to amuse her? Perhaps he sings to her – surely every Irishman sings. Does he murmur endless far-fetched tales of things that befell him back in the Old Country? No one would ever know if they were true, but his wife watches him and tries to smile. Does he comfort her with soft lies about how much better she's looking and how she'll be right as rain in the morning?

There's Bridie standing in the doorway watching them. Old enough to have been with her mother as she went through the travail and pain of birth too many times, and to have watched the deadly exhaustion of yet another mewling newborn sucking the life from her. Bridie thinking, Oh, charm away, Father, but why could you not have spared her? Could you not have deprived yourself of that moment's satisfaction, for her sake?

There are darker possibilities. Connor has a history of having a hot temper, of hitting his pupils. Given the beliefs of the time – that corporal punishment, within reason, was an essential part of child-rearing – it's likely that he hit his own children too. There are those boys of his with the broken bones, after all. He might have hit his wife. Hit his daughter. The times allowed a man to do pretty much what he liked in the privacy of his own home. While her mother was alive, Bridie might have put up with it, mother and daughter supporting each other, protecting each other. That's not hard to imagine. Then, with Ann dead, that unhappy violent house might have become unbearable.

Or – could it be about *Mrs Hazlett my housekeeper*? I think she'd have lived in the house after Ann's death, to be able to get up to the little ones in the night. She might have slept on a stretcher in the kitchen. Then one morning, the sun not quite up, Bridie's coming back from the outhouse and sees Mrs Hazlett slipping out of her father's bedroom.

But perhaps the story isn't about *his* behaviour, but *hers*. Was Joseph Connor the helpless father of a wild, wilful girl? A girl full of passionate rages, out of control, reckless, defiant, promiscuous? Prancing out of home and into the pub as a way of getting back at a long-suffering father trying to rein her in? That's certainly not the story I've been telling myself. There were all those exams passed in double-quick time. Those parents eager for her to teach their children. Not to mention the look of her in those photos. For the sake of completeness and fairness I have to audition the possibility of Bridie as a wild and wicked girl, but my heart's not in it.

Whatever these few letters might or might not reveal about Bridie, they certainly shine a hard bright light backwards onto her father. There are few facts to be found in these cautious letters, but one thing is beyond doubt: Joseph Connor deliberately precipitated trouble for his daughter. He didn't have to tell Inspector Elliott that his daughter was boarding at the hotel, something that implied immoral behaviour that the Department could never condone. He didn't have to urge him to *remove* her – which could mean remove her to another school, but it could also mean remove her from the Service altogether. Bridie's life at Terrible Vale was a good one. A removal, even to another school, could only be a step backwards. And if she was sacked, what future could she have?

If Connor hadn't written the letter, it might have been weeks before the Inspector learned about Miss Connor's irregular behaviour. Connor must have known that sending the letter would force the Inspector's hand, resulting in a cascade of consequences that could only be bad for his daughter. It looks like a hateful, punishing thing to do, the act of a man carried away by self-righteous rage and a hot determination to do damage.

If I'd read these letters at the start of this whole thing, I'd have read the file very differently. I'd have skipped all the ups and downs I've been feeling about Joseph Connor, one moment leaping to his defence, the next agreeing with his accusers. There'd have been no doubt in my mind, because a man who could treat his daughter as harshly as this was capable of all the other things he'd been accused of. Instead of having a pro-Connor-shaped hole at the start, and having to keep trying to squeeze the file through it, I'd have fed everything I discovered through an *anti*-Connor-shaped hole.

It's been uncomfortable sitting with all that uncertainty. I feel a little rush of satisfaction. I've got the story straight now. Joseph Connor really was a bad man.

27th July 1896
Parents at Terrible Vale to Inspector Elliott

Dear Sir, in re. Miss Connor's removal from here, we the undersigned parents of the children attending the

Terrible Vale Provisional school respectfully ask you to reconsider the matter.

She has given every satisfaction and the children all like her and would much rather have her than a stranger.

If her removal was a promotion we would have been glad to see her get it but as it is not we hope you will favourably consider our petition and allow her to remain.

We are, dear sir, yours respectfully
John Boyd
William Hughes
Charles Neil
Richard Dillon
Edward Sheather

Gossip about Bridie Connor leaving home and living at the pub would surely have travelled like red-hot lava from neighbour to neighbour. These men don't seem to know the full story, but they know that she hasn't applied for a transfer, that this isn't what she wants. Whatever they've heard, it can't have been anything terrible about Bridie, because they still want her to teach their children.

But it's taken ten days for the parents to see what's happened and make this appeal. By the time they do, it's too late.

28th July 1896
Inspector Elliott to the Chief Inspector

Although the attached petition speaks well for Miss Connor, lately teacher at Terrible Vale, I do not think it would be advisable to sanction what the residents ask for. As explained in my memo of 17th inst, Miss Connor is boarding at a hotel close to her father's home. Since writing my last memo I have visited Currabubula and found that there is not the slightest hope of a reconciliation between Miss Connor and her father. The dispute must have an injurious effect on both schools, and Miss Connor would be much better away from the hotel. None of the petitioners are willing to let her board with them.

I recommend that the residents of Terrible Vale be informed (through Mr John Boyd) that Miss Connor's removal to Mullaley has been sanctioned in her own interest, and that the Minister is unable to allow her to stop at Terrible Vale.

A.E.

In all the many letters by Inspector Elliott in the file, this is the only one in which I hear anything approaching feeling. *Not the slightest hope of a reconciliation.* There's a tone of frustration, of intentions thwarted, as if he's tried to bring about a reconciliation and been unable to. There's not just *no hope* of a reconciliation, there's *not the slightest hope*. The petition *speaks well for Miss Connor.* The transfer has been arranged *in her own interest.* To my ear this all sounds sympathetic. I think he knows what's happened, and he knows that Bridie is the innocent party.

The puzzling heart of the whole situation lies in this sentence: *None of the petitioners are willing to let her board with them.* If she could have boarded anywhere other than the pub, there'd have been no reason to send her away. Surely if those petitioners knew that, they'd have worked something out. Was there really no lean-to they could make habitable? No verandah that could be enclosed as a sleepout? They wanted to keep her as their teacher, but couldn't do the one thing that would have made that possible.

I'm wondering if the Inspector might have his own reasons for not spelling out the accommodation situation to these families. It might be a problem he doesn't want solved. If Bridie stays in the neighbourhood, the warring father and daughter will go on being a scandal and that *injurious effect on both schools* will continue. Putting an end to that has to be the Inspector's priority, and the only way to do that is to send Miss Connor far, far away.

Mullaley Provisional School

Mullaley is a tiny speck on the map, a longish way west of Gunnedah, out in the black soil country where summers are an endless scorching of the shimmering hot plain and winters turn everything into sticky black mud. For anyone travelling from Currabubula in 1896, it was a tediously extended journey, requiring a change of trains and the last couple of hours by road in a coach. It was hardly even a village, just a hotel, a blacksmith, a few scattered houses and the small stark wooden room that was the school.

The file for Mullaley Provisional School makes painful reading. Every teacher sent there was soon begging for a transfer. Mullaley is too remote, they say. In winter the road is impassable for months on end. The climate's harsh. The locals are hostile. Several times the Inspector tells the Department that he is *unable to nominate a teacher* there. Uriah Burgess, Bridie's predecessor at Mullaley, had been transferred there from Newcastle. He'd gone reluctantly, and only because a teacher who refused a transfer would be sacked.

This is where, three weeks after her father writes to the Inspector, Miss B. Connor takes up her new posting. As the previous teachers had done, she lodges with Mrs Davies at the Post Office, a hundred yards from the school. Inspector Elliott may or may not have realised that the Post Office was part of the hotel, which was actually called the Post Office Hotel. Miss Connor, sent away from Currabubula because she couldn't live in one hotel, is now living in another.

At Currabubula and Terrible Vale, Bridie had been living among people who'd known her since she was a child, people – certainly in the case of Terrible Vale – who liked and respected her. Now she's living among strangers in a place every previous teacher had been desperate to leave. Inspector Elliott might say *the removal to Mullaley is in her own interest*, but it could only be the bitterest exile for her. Each morning, walking to the school, seeing the handful of buildings that made up her new world and the vast lonely plain in all directions around it, she feels punished, far beyond whatever her crime had been in her father's eyes.

A month after Bridie Connor takes over at Mullaley, Inspector Elliott visits the school, perhaps for the first time.

28th September 1896
From Inspector Elliott to the Chief Inspector

Sir, the building at Mullaley has never been painted, and it is consequently unsightly and likely to fall into disrepair. Some minor improvements are also required. I recommend that I be permitted to have the work carried out at a cost of 10 pounds.

A. Elliott, Quirindi

A month later, Miss Connor asks his advice.

21st October 1896
Bridget Connor to Inspector Elliott

Sir, I have the honour to apply for information concerning the painting of the school. Will I close the school whilst being painted, and for how long?

I have etc.
Bridget Connor

Miss Connor: Mr Purcell must carry out his contract by interfering with the school work as little as possible. If he says it is necessary to close the school for more than one day, he must let you know at least a week beforehand when and for how long he wants the room, so that you may receive sanction to discontinue work.

A.E.

Bridie's appeal is abrupt, as well as being uncharacteristically ungrammatical. This is a person in a panic. She needs help, and not just about the length of time she should close the school.

Inspector Elliott gives her careful, explicit instructions. He doesn't hide behind the passive voice, as so many of these official letters do, but addresses her directly: *you*. It's almost a fatherly tone I'm hearing. And he's going out of his way to help her. For a start, he's made the trek out to Mullaley. That gives her the small gift of a familiar face and a sense that she hasn't been cast into the outer darkness and forgotten. It gives her a chance for her to speak to someone who knows the truth about her situation. I'm trying to imagine their conversation. Where would it happen? In the schoolroom perhaps, after the pupils have gone home. But in 1896 a private meeting between a young woman and a man might have seemed what we'd now call *inappropriate*, so they probably meet in some public but respectable room of the Post Office Hotel, the dining room perhaps: the distant clink of glasses from out in the bar, that smell of old beer and dust. He'd choose his words carefully, of course. But by a tone of voice, a glance, a carefully calibrated smile, he could offer her some comfort.

As well as that, he's going to get her schoolroom fixed up, and he isn't going to wait for her to beg for it to be done, the way Joseph Connor has had to beg for every repair. He's seen what was needed, and he's making the request. He's doing the organising, too. He's not expecting Bridie to find someone who'll do the work, and then go through the whole palaver of tenders and haggling, the way her father's always had to do. Instead, he's asked around and found Mr Purcell. He's done the haggling on Bridie's behalf. If there are problems, Purcell is to bring them to the Inspector.

These bland little notes aren't much, but they're the nearest thing to evidence that I'm likely to find about why Bridie had to be sent away. Within the very narrow scope of what's possible, the Inspector is going out of his way to help her and support her. I don't think he'd do that unless he was sympathetic to her plight. I think he knows what's happened between the father and the daughter, and he knows it's the father who's done wrong.

He might have been *allied with* Connor on earlier occasions, as A.W. Brown and John Bradbury claimed. If he was, it might have been that he needed teachers so badly that he was prepared to turn a blind eye to their shortcomings. But the blow-up between father and daughter has shifted his attitude. Joseph Connor had the power to hurt his daughter, and now – using the Inspector as his weapon – he's gone ahead and hurt her.

Through Long Illness and Misfortune

While Bridie is coming to terms with her new life, Joseph Connor's trail in the Currabubula file continues as if nothing has happened. He applies for two new chairs for the schoolroom to replace the worn-out ones and it only takes an exchange of four letters – plus tenders, of course – to get them. He applies for a pair of gates for the schoolyard. His daughter has been wrenched out of her life, her present happiness destroyed and her future sabotaged, exiled in a sad lonely place, but he's sitting pretty on his new Austrian chairs, purchase cost 7 shillings each, and writing tidy letters to the Department asking for permission to act as secretary for the trustees of the Currabubula Common.

4th January 1897
Inspector Elliott to the Chief Inspector

I recommend that Mr Connor be permitted to act as Secretary to the trustees of the Currabubula Common.
He can perform the duties without interfering with his ordinary duty, and he is not paid for the work.

A.E.

Note: J. Connor present address: the Hospital, Tamworth.

The last we heard of Joseph Connor's health was that *dangerous attack of the pleurisy* two years earlier. Now, five months later, he's in hospital, and not just overnight.

This is his last letter. He's too ill to hold the pen. Ernest writes the letter from his father's dictation.

19th June 1897
Joseph Connor to Chief Inspector Bridges

Sir,
I have the honour to apply for either six months' sick leave or retirement from the Service. To this application I attach a medical certificate from Dr Harmon of Quirindi and another from Dr Crisp of Tamworth. The condition in which I find myself is that I am unable to leave my bed, nor have I been able to leave it for a month.

Through long illness and misfortune and the expense of building a new house, into which to remove my family, I have exhausted all my money. My new house is now approaching completion, and we will be removing into it in the course of a few days.

Having no means, I do not know in the world what to do for my large family of motherless little children, and I appeal to the Minister to grant me some salary or else sanction my retirement from the service.

I am in an exceedingly weak condition, and the worry and anxiety caused by the uncertainty of my present position, tends to make me much worse than I would be otherwise.

As Mr Elliott is absent inspecting on the plains, I have, to save delay, taken the liberty of addressing the letter to you, Sir.

I have etc.
J. Connor, per E. Connor.

For the first time he sounds very Irish. *I do not know in the world what to do.* You can hear his voice, hear the despair. He's very alone. There's no wife to help him. No adult children. Bridie is estranged and far away. Alfred is far away too – he's finished his stint as pupil-teacher to his father and has been assigned to distant Heron's Creek school. The only child Connor can look to for help is Ernest, but he's only seventeen.

What a cry from the heart this is, in a file of cool official correspondence. It's impossible not to sympathise, and I do. But my heart has hardened against Joseph Connor. Sympathy is overlaid with a sense that he's getting what was coming to him. If he hadn't caused his daughter to be sent away, she'd be there beside him. He'd have comfort in his illness. He'd know that his children weren't completely motherless. He might even have listened when she steered him away from *exhausting all his money* on the new house. His life has veered into an awful mess, and it's his own doing.

A month later, Bridie visits. It's probably the winter school holiday and it sounds as if she was in Currabubula for some time, perhaps the full two weeks of the break.

11th July 1897
Bridget Connor to Inspector Elliott

Sir, I regret having to apply for leave of absence on Monday, 12th Inst.

My father is very ill, and on Friday night (the night I intended to return to Mullaley), he expressed a wish that I should remain in Currabubula till Sunday. I did so, but was unable to get to Werris Creek on Sunday night to catch the North Western mail train, as the luggage train from the north was some hours late, and it was raining too heavily for me to drive to Werris Creek.

I was therefore compelled to wait till Monday for a train, and I hope, Sir, that under these circumstance, I may be excused.

I have etc.
B.C.

Miss Connor: Absence on 12th inst sanctioned.
A.E.

This is beyond sad. In July 1896 there was *no possibility of a reconciliation* between the father and daughter. A year later some sort of reconciliation has happened. How terrible to have lost that year of time that the two of them could have shared. How tragic that it's only now, with Connor on his deathbed, that they can come together again. Too late, too late. What a waste. What a fool Joseph Connor has been.

Expressed a wish. Behind those bland words lies an ocean of feeling. Was Connor able to speak the words of painful regret, painful remorse? Were the two of them able to put words to their sorrow, or was it an unspoken peacemaking, a matter of a look and a touch?

Two weeks later, Joseph Connor makes his will.

23rd July 1897
This is the last will and testament of me, Joseph Connor, Public School Teacher of Currabubula in the colony of New South Wales.

I hereby bequeath to my children Abigail Sophia Connor, Adolphus Benjamin Connor, Louis Charles Connor, Beatrice Ada Connor and Tristram Cedric Connor the whole of my property both real and personal for the purpose of rearing and educating them, but as soon as any and each one of them shall be able to earn his or her livelihood, they shall no longer receive support from my estate, which consists of three blocks of land situated at Currabubula, together with all moneys in my name in the Bank of New South Wales Tamworth, also my horses cattle dray harness and any other property whatever which may be in my name at the time of my death after my funeral expenses and all my lawful debts will have been paid and I hereby appoint Hope Gould storekeeper of Currabubula, and William Bollard Junior of Duri farmer as Executors for carrying the provisions of this will. To these executors I hereby delegate the power of managing the estate according to their judgement, as well as full control over the children named in the will.

signed, J. Connor, Testator
Witness: James O'Laughlin, Teacher
Agnes Lindley, servant

Dated at Currabubula this 23rd day of July 1897

The three blocks of land were together worth 135 pounds. The five horses were worth 37 pounds. He had 500 pounds in the bank – the equivalent of about eighteen months' salary. The most valuable single item in the probate list was the piano, worth 20 pounds. A piano! Suddenly there's a picture of aspirational striving, a piano as a mark of a superior social standing. But really, who in that household had time to play the piano?

Joseph Connor doesn't mention his three oldest children in the will. Understandable enough, I suppose. The older ones are earning.

They can take care of themselves. Still, as I know from my own life, it's a chilly thing not to be mentioned in your father's will. Could there not have been some lawyerly phrase about *Notwithstanding my affection for my children Bridget Connor, Alfred Connor and Ernest Connor ...?* After all, a will is a kind of posthumous message to your children. You have to organise the money side of things, of course. But couldn't Joseph Connor have given his adult children the small loving gesture of being named and acknowledged?

I'm wondering what it means that he's appointed two local men to manage his estate and take *full control* of his young children. He has three adult children who might be thought the obvious ones to take care of their little brothers and sisters. Obviously he trusts Gould and Bollard, but he'd have known that the money would run out before long, and could he be sure that the executors would go on supporting the children then?

Another way of organising it would surely have been to make the older children guardians of the young ones, and to put the money in trust for their upkeep. You could almost think that Joseph Connor trusted those two townspeople more than he trusted his three older children.

Three weeks later no one had to mince words about Joseph Connor's illness.

17th August 1897
Bridget Connor to Inspector Elliott

Sir, I regret having to apply for leave of absence from 17th August to 27th Aug, inclusive.

My father is in a dying state in the Tamworth hospital, and as the doctors think he can live only a short time, and as my school is some distance from Tamworth, I should like to remain near him for a few days.

I am very sorry that I could not have remained at my school till leave of absence was sanctioned, but as I was telegraphed for, I was forced to leave my school without first applying to you for permission.

I sincerely trust that I may be excused, and that the leave of absence I have asked for will be granted.

I have etc.

B.C.

The Chief Inspector: In consequence of the serious illness of Miss Connor's father, I recommend that her absence from duty, and the closing of the school under her charge, from 17th to 27th August, '97, inclusive, be sanctioned.

A.E.

25th Aug 1897
Inspector Elliott to the Chief Inspector

Telegram

Connor formerly head teacher dead will you allow school to close tomorrow

Joseph Connor was fifty-two. Even for those times, that's an early death. I'm assuming he died of TB – it had killed his wife, after all, and there'd been that *dangerous attack of the pleurisy*.

At this point the obvious thing would have been for Bridie to resign, return to Currabubula and look after the family. She hadn't done so when Ann died and she didn't do so now. Instead, her brother

Alfred gave up his good position at Heron's Creek Public School. He applied for a transfer to Terrible Vale Provisional in order to care for the children. Professionally it was a big step backwards. Meanwhile Bridie, on half his salary, stayed on at the dead-end of Mullaley. Families have all sorts of ways to cope with a crisis, but this does seem an odd way of going about things.

Bridie lasted a year at Mullaley. Then she applied to be transferred. Over the next four years she was posted to eight other schools in different parts of country New South Wales. Then, in 1901, she resigned and married. And the man she married? None other than the publican to whose hotel she'd gone that day in 1896, George Morris.

Aha! Mystery solved! He must have been the *reason to believe* that her father had found so intolerable. But no, that doesn't work. At the time of the bust-up, Morris was thirty-seven, a widower with five children. Well-off, the leading man in the community. Why would Connor have objected to George Morris as a son-in-law? True, he was Protestant, but did Joseph Connor really feel so strongly about keeping his daughter in the faith? In any case, at twenty-one Bridie didn't need her father's permission to marry. Why wait five years?

Over the next ten years George and Bridie had five children. George died in 1925 and Bridie went on running the hotel with one of her sons until a few years before she died in 1939, at sixty-five.

There's a photo of her taken in about 1930. Behind a majestic bosom and little round scholarly glasses, there's the woman who, some three decades before, had made a life for herself as the teacher at Terrible Vale, liked and respected by pupils and parents. And known only to the mind packed away under that tidy hair is the reason why, one day in 1896, she put a few essentials in a bag and – from courage, or desperation, or something else – *left her home*.

One Last Turn

Nearly a decade after I'd first seen the Currabubula school file I still couldn't see a story in it, but at the same time I couldn't seem to abandon it. *There's something here*, I kept telling myself. *I just can't see what it is.* Now I was turning through the many bits of paper I'd generated, trying to bring myself to say a final goodbye to the material so I could move on.

Tucked away and hidden between some other papers, I unearthed a scribbled note I'd made on my very first trip to the Archives. I'd stumbled on the forged letters denouncing Joseph Connor and I'd jotted down this note because I was interested in complaints against a teacher, and here was another complaint against another teacher. But the date – 1911 – put it far beyond Connor's time, so once I started to delve more deeply into his letters I'd put the note away and forgotten about it.

Back then I didn't know who *Mrs G. Morris* was. Now I knew that she was Bridie Connor.

Aug 1911
Complaint by Mrs G. Morris against teacher.

> Son is in second class under Miss Sawyer, Asst. Mrs M. belittled teacher in hearing of child. Reflections on the teacher most unmerited, but are characteristic of the person who makes them.
>
> This woman is always maligning teachers. When I first visited Currabubula, her complaint was that both of the teachers were R.C. Now she has changed her tune.
>
> Her accusations are not sufficient to warrant further action.
>
> In regard to her letter: she was a teacher in the Dept. Accuses the present teacher of being slipshod. A tone of ridicule. Wants more up-to-date intellectual man for a change.
>
> Attendance 50.5 but only accommodation for 36 in the larger room – the 2 rooms both have to be used – so need for an Assistant Teacher. But accomm a problem. Notwithstanding the high tariff at the Hotel, it is not a suitable place for a female teacher to stay at. In addition Mrs Morris, wife of the proprietor, refuses to take a lady boarder.

So Bridie was attacking the teacher just as she'd watched her father being attacked! She was refusing to *take a lady boarder*, when that was exactly what had triggered disaster for her! She was belittling a teacher with a *tone of ridicule*, accusing them of being *slipshod* and not *intellectual* enough! She was even complaining that *both the teachers were R.C.*, when she'd grown up Roman Catholic herself! Bridie had escaped, married a wealthy man, had a good life. She should have been sympathetic to the ones still in the world she'd scrambled out of. But here she was, lashing out at them. I couldn't understand where this awful woman had suddenly come from.

Or had she been there all along? This other Bridie – harsh, contemptuous, a bully who enjoyed *maligning* people – maybe she'd always been the real Bridie. I hadn't had much to work on with her: a handful of letters and a few sketchy facts. It had been easy to make a simple picture of her, with none of the light and shade I'd been forced to add to my picture of her father. Now I have to rethink what might have happened on that June night in 1896. The Bridie I've been picturing wouldn't have done anything to cause the confrontation with her father, but this sneering bully might have. Was that catastrophic falling-out her fault, rather than her father's?

Which takes me back to Joseph Connor. I have a niggling feeling of not being finished with him, and I decide to send away for his death certificate. Under *Cause of Death* it doesn't say *Tuberculosis*, as I'd expected, but *Spinal Caries*. I went online and found that spinal caries is in fact tuberculosis, but a particularly awful kind. The bacteria get into the spine and slowly destroy it. There's nothing romantic or glamorous about it. This isn't a lovely woman singing her heart out while she dies. It's not Keats writing masterpieces between coughs. This is the spine being eaten away nerve by shrieking nerve.

And it's slow. Tuberculosis of the spine starts in the lungs and it takes time to spread to the spine. Joseph Connor had needed a spell in hospital for that *dangerous attack of the pleurisy* two years before he died. If that was TB, he'd have already been ill then, and he wouldn't have got any better over the next two years. When he fired off the letter that derailed his daughter's life, he only had twelve months to live. By then the disease would have invaded his spine. The letter would have been written by a tormented human being out of his mind with pain.

Or else he was in the grip of the one thing that could have relieved pain in 1897: some form of opium. Opium can do bad things to the way you think. You can be convinced that people are against you when they aren't, or that they've done terrible things when they haven't. No amount of reasoning can persuade you.

Either way, maddened by pain or by a drug, a person in that state would be more than capable of doing something they shouldn't have done. Joseph Connor shouldn't have fired off that letter to the Inspector. In fact there were a lot of things he shouldn't have done. But alongside those things I have to set this new fact, the drawn-out agony of his death. It doesn't change everything I've decided about him, but it casts a different, more merciful light. The note about Bridie's complaints does the reverse. I'd idealised her. Now I have to accept that she might have been an arrogant troublemaker.

How satisfying it had been to swell with righteous indignation about Joseph Connor, and with warm outrage on Bridie's behalf. Out of vivid feelings, how easy to make a story. Now that I've seen Joseph Connor's death certificate, and the report about Bridie, I can't unsee them. I'm obliged to add what they tell me to all the other things I've learned about those two people. But how much less pleasurable it is to be plunged back into uncertainties, ambiguities, all the what-ifs of this conversation with the past.

Where does that leave these pages of exploration? At the start of this long trail through the Currabubula school file I thought there'd be a story between the lines of all those documents. Who was Joseph Connor, and what had happened between him and his neighbours? But trying to make sense of these scraps of the past has been like grabbing at water. Stories floated up but then sank again. Characters came forward as one thing but on a second look turned into something else. Meanings took shape, then evaporated. My sympathies, like a school of fish, wheeled towards Joseph Connor. With the next letter they gathered, regrouped, wheeled the other way.

But the journey into that world was as irresistible as gobbling up a detective story. I'd turned corner after corner listening for the clue that would piece everything together, always hopeful that the next turn would reward me with the satisfaction of certainty. I'm shocked at how sure I'd been, each time I thought I'd finally arrived at a judgement.

I can see now that those judgements haven't really come from the file. There was a lot of detail there – enough, I'd thought at the start, to construct a true picture of the people and what they'd done. But each one had to be interpreted. Was the word *compelled* as significant as it had sounded to me, or was it just a casual choice? And no matter how many letters there were, they would only ever be a partial record – and in fact no amount of detail would ever fill in every corner of the life behind them. There'd been a time when I'd fantasised about finding some kind of private journal that Joseph Connor might have kept. But even that wouldn't tell the whole story. It would only be what he chose to write down. It would still have to be weighed up before being delared true or false, or somewhere in between. But weighed up against what? How had I weighed up the documents in the file?

Standing back from the close-up passion of the chase, I can see now that I've been drawing on what we all draw on when evidence is patchy or unreliable: ourselves. I've brought to bear my beliefs, my preconceptions and prejudices, and all my unconscious biases. The picture's been shaped by everything I know and everything I don't know. By my memories and my imagination, by invention and speculation. I'd pored over that picture of Bridie in the school photograph, a young woman turning away and glancing down, and I'd given her the feeling I might have had in her position – resistance to a pre-ordained destiny. I'd drawn on my memory of my grandmother, her life shaped and shrunken by her domineering father – *Over my dead body!* – and I'd cast Bridie's father in the same mould. I'd drawn on my experiences of being at school, the teachers I'd had and my fellow pupils, the dramas of all those tug-of-warring personalities. I'd called up stereotypes and things out of novels: stern fathers, powerless women, narrow small-town horizons turning into persecution.

All that had given me a way to make sense out of the letters and to arrive at something resembling a story. But the truth is, it was a fragile little construction. Turning over one more piece of paper – Joseph Connor's death certificate or Bridie's complaint about the teacher – was enough to make it collapse.

Watching myself watching Joseph Connor, I'm starting to see that the real puzzle here isn't actually about him. It's about the person who's been doing the watching. Why have I cared so much? What was the compulsion I felt as I forensically analysed each cool little missive? What was the feeling of fulfilment when I came up with a way of explaining what they contained? And why had I found it so hard to change my mind each time another document obliged me to take a different view?

Something was going on, and it wasn't just a writer trying to nose out a story. It was something perhaps we all share: a craving for the pleasure of certainty. Of course I'd wanted to make a story out of the letters in the Currabubula school file. It's what humans do. We prune the complexities out of a situation and lop off the awkward contradictions. We foreground some details and shrink others so the events seem to line up. Reflecting on my own dogged hunt for the story in the file, I'm starting to see it as a small-scale model of how all of us go about being in the world. Making a story gives us a way to make meaning out of the overwhelming mass of stuff that life presents us with. Otherwise we'd be panicked, or paralysed. Certainty steadies the wobble of all that we're not sure about.

The flipside of that comfort is that uncertainty can feel like an existential threat. That's why, once I'd made my story, I was inclined to stick to it no matter what. I can see how that could make for a kind of us-and-them situation, where others who arrive at the same story belong to one tribe and those who arrive at a different one become strangers or even enemies.

What this last turn of the story is telling me is to forgo the pleasure and reassurance of conviction. It's reminding me that outside the neatly trimmed parkland of story is the wild unfenced landscape of the real. No matter how high a hill I might climb to understand Joseph Connor or his daughter, I can never see everything. A different hill would give me a different perspective – just as true and just as partial. The vast enfolded landscape out there is real enough, but any judgement about it can only be provisional. The best map is a mind open to other possibilities.

We love resolving uncertainties, but a stronger necessity might be to live with them. My long crooked journey through the Currabubula school file has invited me to embrace something not as cosy as a story but more true: the uncurated, unexplained, unshaped, enigmatically fascinating moral mystery of people living out their days in the complicated world we share.

A Note on Sources

The documents and photograph reproduced here can be found in the NSW State Archives Collection at Museums of History NSW (MHNSW-StAC: NRS-3829 [5/15627.2] and HMNSW-StAC: NRS-15051-1-10 [553]-1). My warm thanks go to the staff there who assisted me with unfailing patience and expertise.

This isn't a complete record of all the documents that are in the file – it's a selection – but where I've used documents, I've generally reproduced them verbatim. My aim was to let them speak for themselves as far as possible.

There are just a few instances where, to avoid repetition and drawn-out exchanges, I've merged and streamlined a number of documents.

When I've intervened in this way, I haven't invented anything and I've taken care not to alter the meaning or tone of the originals. The documents speak more briskly, but still speak with their own voices.

Small, non-significant details of spelling and punctuation have been edited for consistency, but where errors or inconsistencies reveal something about the writer (for example John Bradbury's unconventional spelling and grammar), I've retained them.

The man named here as Joseph Connor, and his family and neighbours, were all real people. I've drawn a picture of them based on my interpretation of the documents, but that picture is the work of my imagination. For that reason, I've changed the names of all the people in the file. No great detective work would be needed to identify them, but in changing the names I'm making it clear that this odd hybrid isn't history or biography, and that the picture I've drawn of those people may not have much resemblance to the actual individuals who lived in Currabubula at the end of the nineteenth century.

This is a book about how we make stories out of limited information. I've made one kind of story out of the information in the file, but one of the reasons for including the real documents is so that readers have the chance to make their own. Another set of life experiences, another personality, another worldview . . . a different story.